4

# THE COUNTER-ARMADA, 1596

*The Journall of the 'Mary Rose'*

Stephen and
Elizabeth Usherwood

# The Counter-Armada, 1596

*The Journall of the 'Mary Rose'*

**THE BODLEY HEAD**
LONDON SYDNEY
TORONTO

British Library Cataloguing
in Publication Data

The Counter-armada, 1596: the Journall of the Mary Rose.
1. Howard of Effingham, Charles Howard, *Baron*
2. Cadiz (Spain)—History—Philip II, 1556–1598
I. Usherwood, Stephen    II. Usherwood, Elizabeth
III. Carew, *Sir* George
946'88   DP 302.C23
ISBN 0–370–30556–6

Printed in Great Britain for
The Bodley Head Ltd
9 Bow Street, London WC2E 7AL
by Redwood Burn Limited, Trowbridge
Set in Linotron 202 Plantin
by Wyvern Typesetting Limited, Bristol
*First published 1983*

To Geoffrey Bill
without whose scholarship
and generosity this book
could not have been written

# Contents

Introduction, 9

I. Leave of the Queen, 15

II. Our now set-out Army, 25

III. What enterprise was fittest, 52

IV. Assured of the Victory, 76

V. No enemy to make resistance, 98

VI. Her Majesty's pleasure, 108

VII. Everyone taking his own course, 118

Appendix I A journall (original text of the journal with corrections as made by Sir George Carew), 124

II Journal of Jan van Doornik (translation of a log book kept for part of the voyage by the Admiral of Holland's kinsman), 159

III Tonnage measurements, 165

IV Calendar of English ships named in the *Mary Rose* journal, 166

V Portraits of Sir George Carew, first Earl of Totnes, 170

Index, 174

# List of Plates

*between pages* 48 and 49
1. George Carew, Kt., 1st Earl of Totnes
2. Page from the *Mary Rose* Journal
3. Charles, Lord Howard of Effingham
4. Robert Devereux, 2nd Earl of Essex
5. Sir Francis Vere
6. John Donne

*between pages* 80 and 81
7. Astronomical ring
8. Pocket Dial of the Earl of Essex
9. The Channel coast between Portland and Plymouth
10. Sir Walter Raleigh and his son
11. Jan van Duivenvoorde, Admiral of Holland

*between pages* 112 and 113
12. Title page of the works of St. Gregory of Nyssa
13. Coast of Andalusia showing Cadiz
14. Sir George Carew, miniature by Nicholas Hilliard
15. Head of Philip II

# Introduction

On Thursday, 3 June 1596, an Anglo-Dutch fleet, numbering over 120 vessels, sailed out of Plymouth Sound on a secret mission. It carried 6,000 soldiers, English and Dutch, the largest and best equipped army that had up to that time left these shores. The joint commanders were Charles, Lord Howard of Effingham, the Admiral of the English fleet that defeated the Spanish Armada in 1588, and the young Earl of Essex, who had seen active service against Spain in the Netherlands, France and Portugal. The Dutch contingent of twenty-four ships was headed by the Admiral of Holland, Jan van Duivenvoorde, Lord of Warmond, a hero of the Dutch war of independence. Every captain received, on the eve of departure, sealed instructions with strict orders not to open them unless separated from the fleet by foul weather. These named Cadiz, the largest of the Spanish Atlantic ports, as their objective. After a three-week voyage and one day's action by sea and land the harbour and town were in the allies' hands. They stayed a fortnight and then sailed for home, laden with spoil and bringing two captured Spanish galleons as prizes.

Hitherto there has been no objective account of this once-famous exploit. Some have called it 'a summer's bravery' and others 'the greatest scandal of the age'. The key to its true history lies in a thirty-eight-page manuscript, part of a volume marked *Voyages*, in the library of the Archbishop of Canterbury's palace at Lambeth, headed *A Journall of all the particularities that fell out in the voyage under the charge of the Lord Admiral . . .* This is a log with entries made from day to day between Easter Sunday 1596, when the author took leave of the Queen at Greenwich and went to join his ship at Dover, and 7 August, when he brought her back to Plymouth. He neither signed it, nor gave the name of his ship, and for that reason Admiral Sir Julian Corbett, who saw the manuscript

9

at the end of the last century when writing his *Successors of Drake*, concluded it was an edited copy of an account by a person of no great importance. But recently it was examined by the Archbishop's librarian at Lambeth, Dr. Geoffrey Bill, who, with the weight of his great authority, identified the handwriting as that of Sir George Carew, who is known from State documents to have been Master of Ordnance for the whole of the English sea and land forces, captain of the *Mary Rose*, a Queen's ship, and member of the Council of War presided over by Howard and Essex. Sir George, a Devon man, first cousin to Sir Walter Raleigh, and a prolific writer on the history of Ireland, subsequently held high command at the time of the great rebellion by O'Neil, Earl of Tyrone. A large archive of his papers was deposited at Lambeth by Archbishop Sheldon, a member of Charles II's Privy Council, and has remained there ever since. Sir George's Cadiz journal, which was never treated as part of this archive, may have come into the hands of the Archbishops of Canterbury much earlier, possibly in 1596, when John Whitgift was Primate; he was the second most important person in the Privy Council, responsible for censoring all printed matter, since he licensed the printers. The Cecils were determined that only one short official account of the operation should be published. Sir George may have surrendered his journal to the Archbishop, and it was only after his authorship had been recognised by Dr. Bill that its unique importance as an historical document became clear. Raleigh's high-flown description of the naval action in Cadiz harbour was not published till, long after his execution, his grandson found it among his papers. Other contemporary accounts of the campaign, Hakluyt's, for example, were written in the form of essays, summarising, with hindsight, the course of events and so giving the impression that victory was easily won. Any unedited record of a combined operation in the sixteenth century would be a rarity, but Sir George's vivid prose recreates the excitement of hazards at sea, storms, fog, sudden calm; men of an assault force drowning in breakers as they make for the shore in open boats; and an enemy galleon with her crew still on board, burning to the waterline, a scene sharply etched in an epigram by John Donne, then a young volunteer on Essex's flagship, shaken by his first experience of war's terrifying reality.

The Queen, on receiving the first report of the victory, brought home in advance by Sir Antony Ashley, wrote to Howard and Essex: 'You have made me famous, dreadful and renowned, not more for your victory than for your courage, nor more for either than for such plentiful liquor of mercy. Never was heard in so few days of so great a work achieved. Let the army know I care not so much for being Queen as that I am sovereign of such subjects.'

The fleet's return coincided with a double wedding in which the whole court was interested, that of Lady Elizabeth and Lady Katherine Somerset, the Earl of Worcester's daughters, and the poet Edmund Spenser, who had dedicated *The Faerie Queen* to the sovereign, inserted in his *Prothalamion* for the wedding verses of daringly extravagant praise addressed to the Earl of Essex:

'. . . noble Peer,
Great England's glory and the world's wide wonder
Whose dreadful name late through all Spain did thunder . . .'

This joy and elation rapidly evaporated when the Queen learned that her share of the spoils was not so large as she had anticipated. Orders went out for a thorough inquisition into the value and nature of all the plunder. Sir George, who had been entrusted, before the fleet sailed, with the impossible task of registering everything pillaged and estimating its value, had to supervise this post-mortem and was even accused of having himself profited from the campaign, a charge he indignantly refuted.

A man of forty-two, he had long experience of both land and sea fighting. His father, a Devon man, was simultaneously Dean of Bristol and of Windsor, a notable sign of Elizabeth's favour. George and his elder brother Peter were named after famous members of the family: Sir George Carew who had commanded the *Mary Rose* and gone down with her when she sank in Portsmouth harbour before the eyes of the King; and Sir Peter Carew, soldier, diplomat, musician and friend of Henry VIII. The two boys, living at Windsor, were well known to the Queen from an early age, as they served as pages to her favourite, the Earl of Leicester. George, like his father, was educated at Broadgates Hall, Oxford (now Pembroke College), and during his time there his first cousin,

Walter Raleigh, was at Oriel College. In 1576 he was serving as a soldier in Ireland and, as constable of Leighlin Castle, beat off an attack by Rory Oge O'More. Two years later, like many other Devon men, he took to the sea, joining Walter Raleigh, in the *Falcon*, accompanied by six other ships, on a voyage of purchase (a euphemism for piracy). They may have intended to reach the Caribbean, but had not gone far before they took two prizes. The second-in-command, Henry Knollys, absconded with them and four of the ships. Raleigh and Carew went on as far as the Cape Verde islands, where they ran out of supplies and had to return home. It was an early lesson on the necessity of maintaining strict discipline at sea and of having powerful friends at court, for nobody could touch Henry Knollys; his father was the Queen's Treasurer, and his mother her best friend.

George and Peter Carew, like Raleigh, were again in Ireland in 1580, when Peter was taken prisoner and killed. George avenged him by slaying with his own hands the Irishmen believed to have been responsible. An appointment as one of Her Majesty's Gentlemen-Pensioners came in 1582, and later knighthood from Sir John Perrott, the Lord Deputy in Ireland. In 1587 the Queen granted him the Mastership of Ordnance in Ireland, forcing Sir John to remove his own son from that important office. Raleigh, who had acquired large Irish estates along the Blackwater river, was knighted in recognition of his work in sending out colonists to Virginia, and during the Armada campaign was in charge of the land defences of Devon and Cornwall. At about this time Sir Walter had his portrait painted by the much sought-after miniaturist Nicholas Hilliard, and there is every reason to believe that Sir George did likewise. A splendid example of Hilliard's craft, now in the Victoria and Albert Museum, known only as 'A man clasping a hand from a cloud', is inscribed in Latin and dated by the artist, 1588, but by the eighteenth century the identity of the sitters for this and the Raleigh portrait had been lost. The latter was identified in the 1940's by the Treasurer of Oriel College, C. S. Emden, because of its similarity with a poorly executed miniature in Vienna. The evidence for identifying the man clasping a hand as Sir George is set out in Appendix V. A fine three-quarter-length portrait of him at about seventy years of age hangs in the hall at

Gorhambury, the Hertfordshire seat of the Earls of Verulam, and the National Portrait Gallery has another version.

When recalled from Ireland in 1592 to take up the post of Lieutenant of Ordnance in England, Sir George immediately improved the efficiency of the Ordnance department, so that by 1596 it was able to equip an expedition that he described to Sir Robert Cecil as 'strong enough to abide the proudest fleet that ever swam'. 'The particularities of what fell out' form the core of this book and we are most grateful to Dr. Geoffrey Bill for permission to transcribe and publish them.

Sir George's subsequent career, unlike that of other commanders at Cadiz, was long and prosperous. In 1580 he had married Joyce Clopton of Clopton House near Stratford-on-Avon. (New Place, the house Shakespeare bought there, was a former Clopton property.) James I appointed him Vice-Chamberlain of Queen Anne's household in 1603, and the borough of Hastings elected him to Parliament the following year. Raised to the peerage as Baron Clopton, in 1605, he became a Privy Councillor in 1616, and on the accession of Charles I was created Earl of Totnes in Devon. When, in 1629, he died at his London residence in the Savoy, the Countess took his body to Holy Trinity Church, Stratford-on-Avon, for burial. There she erected a magnificent tomb for them both close to the grave of Shakespeare. Perhaps in life as in death the playwright and the soldier were much closer than has hitherto been imagined. Who more likely than a Master of Ordnance to have inspired the lines:

> 'Farewell the plumed troop, and the big wars
> That make ambition virtue! O, farewell!
> Farewell the neighing steed, and the shrill trump,
> The spirit-stirring drum, the ear-piercing fife,
> The royal banner, and all quality,
> Pride, pomp and circumstance of glorious war!
> And O you mortal engines, whose rude throats
> The immortal Jove's dread clamours counterfeit,
> Farewell!'

# I

# Leave of the Queen

Queen Elizabeth I spent Easter 1596 by the Thames at Greenwich, where her palace lay close to the shore and, every ebb tide, she could see from the windows vessel after vessel putting to sea for trade, adventure or plunder. This was her birthplace, and in the nearby villages of Deptford and Woolwich her father, Henry VIII, had established, over eighty years before, the shipyards where the Royal Navy was born. Everything required for fitting out the Queen's ships, guns and gunpowder, arms and armour, food and drink, could be fetched from no great distance. The Queen and the court were therefore at the centre of naval affairs, but few could have guessed, when she appeared on her way to church this Easter Sunday, how great an enterprise was about to be set in motion.

There were more of the nobility present than on weekdays, a large gathering of counsellors of state, officers of the crown and gentlemen pensioners waiting for the Queen to come out of her private rooms to attend Divine Service. Earls, barons, Knights of the Garter, all richly dressed and bareheaded, escorted her to the chapel, each in order of precedence, two bearing immediately in front of the Queen the sceptre and the sword of state in its scabbard of red velvet studded with gold *fleurs-de-lis*. Her Majesty was not religious, but loved the ceremonies of religion. A crucifix, with wax-lights burning round it, stood in her private chapel. The music for her choir, composed by musicians of the first rank, was sung by boys selected and trained with the greatest artistry. She was dressed, as always, in a manner that drew every eye, a small gold crown surmounting a red-gold wig, a dress sewn with jewels, open to the waist as was customary for unmarried women; the face fair, but wrinkled, for she was in her sixty-third year; lips sunk inwards to a thin line; eyes dark, but pleasant, noticing everything. Here and there one of the bystanders would kneel as the Queen stopped to speak to him. For some she would remove a glove and allow the long jewelled fingers to be kissed. Kneeling was insisted upon as a measure of security. Many could remember how the Dutch leader, William the Silent, an enemy, like the Queen, of the Spanish king Philip II, had been shot dead by a servant, and more recently how a mad monk had stabbed Henry III of France to death. After chapel, dinner was served, and those bringing food to the Queen's table would be ordered to taste it as a precaution against poisoning.

Assassination was only one of the dangers that had thrown its shadow across Elizabeth's path since her accession over thirty-seven years before. For those prepared to abandon the Catholic faith most of that time had been peaceful and prosperous; there had been only one insurrection, the revolt of the Catholic earls of Northumberland and Westmorland in 1569, which had been cruelly repressed, but year by year from across the Channel and the North Sea refugees and traders from France and the Netherlands had brought stories of civil war, atrocities by drunken, unpaid mercenaries and massacres carried out in the name of religion by mobs moved to fury by rumour-mongering fanatics. Seven out of the seventeen Netherlands provinces formerly owing allegiance to Philip II had, after desperate fighting, won a precarious independence. For over ten years of that struggle they had received men, arms and money from England. The King of Spain, hoping to put an end to this support for rebellion, had sent the Armada of 1588 to transport the army of his then Viceroy, the Duke of Parma, to England.

Another armada was now reported to be on the point of departure and, it was feared, might sail to Ireland and join with Catholic rebels there, expel the English and land in Lancashire, always a strongly Catholic area. In 1595 Philip II had sanctioned assistance for the Catholics in Scotland, who claimed that they could seize ports which the Spanish might use against England. In September 1595 envoys were received in Madrid from the Earl of Tyrone, leader of the rebel chieftains of Ulster, whose skill in diplomacy and war had defeated all English attempts to remove him. Tyrone asked for two or three thousand Spanish infantry, and assured the King that, with them, there would be no doubt of success.

At the same time the Spaniards seemed to be tightening their grip on the English Channel. They were in command of Blavet, near La Baule in southern Brittany, and from there galleys crossed to the Cornish coast in 1595 and burnt the villages of Mousehole, Newlyn and Penzance. Such small raids were impossible to predict, but constant effort was made by the Privy Council to collect every scrap of intelligence about Spanish movements. In December of the same year, for example, a Spanish vessel was badly damaged in a storm off the Scillies. The captain and crew of ten beached her on the Carmarthen coast at Laugharne, where they were arrested and interrogated by Sir Thomas Jones and Edward Donnerley, deputy lieutenants of Carmarthen. They had been bound for Blavet, had jettisoned their cargo of wine, and had no other lading nor arms except for two or three old calivers and rapiers and a barrel of small poniards which a Frenchman shipped, pretending it was saffron. No letters nor books were found in the wreck, except a few old Spanish song sheets ruined by water. The King of Spain's ships of war were, they said, at Andalusia and Lisbon; in Brittany many Spanish soldiers were dying of dysentery; and in Spain the Irish had as free traffic as ever, but not the English.[1]

Early in April the Spaniards struck where they were least expected—at Calais. Their army in the Netherlands, led by the Viceroy there, the Cardinal Archduke Albrecht of Austria,[2] suddenly marched to the coast, captured the fort at the mouth of the harbour and drove the garrison out of the town into the citadel.

It was against this background of doubt and anxiety that

'On Easter Day, the 11th of April [1596] about 12 of the clock at night, the Earl of Essex took his leave of the Queen at Greenwich, the Lord Admiral being gone away from the court before him to bring the ships to Dover; the same night also and the same hour I took my leave of Her Majesty.'[3]

This secret, dark and midnight departure of the Earl and of Sir George Carew, whose journal alone records the moment, marked the end of nine months' preparation and the start of a great enterprise of war. Sir George was the Queen's Lieutenant of Ordnance and, not by accident, the ship awaiting him at Dover bore the name *Mary Rose*, previously carried by the pride of Henry VIII's fleet. The King had seen her capsize and sink at Portsmouth in 1545, when her commander, Sir George Carew's uncle, who bore the same name, and some 700 men were drowned. The Carews came from Mohun Ottery in Devon, and Sir Walter Raleigh was first cousin and close friend of the writer of the journal.

The enterprise was under the joint command of two men for whom Elizabeth had great affection. The Lord Admiral, the Queen's cousin and life-long confidant, Charles, Lord Howard of Effingham, had led the English fleet against the Armada of 1588; at sixty, he was still full of energy, and the Queen, fearing for his health if he were to over-exert himself, had ordered her own physician, Dr. Roger Marbecke, to sail with him. The twenty-nine-year-old Earl of Essex, Robert Devereux, had first come to her notice as the stepson of her dearest friend, the Earl of Leicester, in whose army he had served in the Netherlands in 1587. Since then he had fought under Lord Willoughby in France and with Sir Francis Drake on the coast of Portugal and Spain. Only jealous rivals resented his present high command.

The Commission issued to Howard and Essex outlines the objectives of the expedition and the duties of their subordinate commanders:

'. . . By burning of the King of Spain's ships of war in his havens before they should come forth to the seas, and therewith also destroying his magazines of victuals and his munitions for the arming of his navy, to provide that neither the rebels in Ireland should be aided and strengthened, nor yet the King be able, of long time to repair unto, and have any great navy in readiness to offend us.

'And if you cannot understand of any such particular purposes you shall direct your course to such ports where the greatest number of the King's ships of war are and where his provisions are in store; and there you shall use all good means possible to spoil and burn all the said ships, or as many of them as conveniently you may; and also, you shall destroy or get into your possession to our use, as many of the victuals, powder, ordnance, cordage, and all other apparellings for war as you can.

'That being accomplished, if the town belonging to the port where those ships and magazines are hath great riches, and you shall understand that it is not able to defend itself, you may attempt the taking of such a town and possess of the riches thereof. If, after this, you shall hear of the likelihood of the coming from the Indies of any of the King's carracks laden with riches, you shall send away as many of the ships and men as you shall not have need of, to be used to the taking of such carracks, which we must leave to your consideration.

'For the better and more orderly execution of this your commission, and of those former articles comprised in these our instructions, we do ordain that there shall be two persons serving for the seas, and two that are appointed to serve with the forces for land-service to be counsellors to you in our name, that is Lord Thomas Howard and Sir Walter Raleigh, Sir Francis Vere and Sir Conyers Clifford; and to these four we do add Sir George Carew, our lieutenant of ordnance, to make the number of five, whom also we charge by these presents that they will, as they will answer before God, give their counsels to you both without any private respect to either of you, for love or fear, in all actions to be put in question or taken in hand and the same deliberately to debate as the weight of the matter shall require before any resolution be made and before the putting of the matter in action.'[4]

The body set up by this commission was called the Selected Council or Council of War. When necessary it was augmented by the captains and masters. At sea the signals for convening such meetings were as follows:

'When there is a flag of council of the red cross out in the General's ship, half-mast high against the main mizzen, then the Captains and Masters shall repair on board that ship where the flag is so hanged out, and when the flag of arms shall be displayed, then shall the Selected Council only come on board.'[5]

Sir George Carew, at forty-one, had long experience of campaigning in Ireland, first with his uncle, Sir Peter Carew, a soldier of fortune popular with Henry VIII, and later as Lieutenant of Ordnance for Ireland. He was accustomed to keep careful records, and so for ten weeks he wrote daily in his journal, compiling on-the-spot impressions and details, inserting fresh information as it came in, but never destroying his first draft or colouring up an incident. The result is the only account of the campaign undistorted by hindsight.

The practice of appointing joint commanders for amphibious expeditions was well-established, and there were strong practical reasons for it. If the naval side were led by a great sailor, privately owned ships could easily be persuaded to join, since the prospect of prize money was good; if the land forces were in the hands of a man known to be a bold adventurer, he would be followed by 'voluntaries' serving at their own expense, and even bringing their own horses. Among the 600 who flocked to the banner of Essex in 1596, some, eager for honour and glory, made themselves conspicuous with fine clothes, gold braid and splendid weapons; others embarked to escape their creditors; and a few, like the twenty-five-year-old poet John Donne, because they admired Essex's love of literature and the arts, and hoped for his patronage. Shakespeare knew the breed and the fear that they inspired:

'Rash, inconsiderate, fiery voluntaries,
With ladies' faces and fierce dragons' spleens,
Have sold their fortunes at their native homes,
Bearing their birthrights proudly on their backs,
To make a hazard of new fortunes here.'[6]

At sea 'new fortunes' would come by taking prizes; and on land from looting enemy towns. The majority of crews were technically 'pressed' men, dispatched by their home ports on receipt of orders from the Queen, but many were eager recruits whose ships belonged to merchants who frequently fitted them out with ammunition, stores and victuals for a six months' voyage to seek 'their own adventures of purchase', an Elizabethan euphemism for piracy. The leadership of the Lord High Admiral was warmly welcomed, even though his destination was unknown, because, in contrast to what the Queen and Burghley proclaimed to the world, his purpose was clearly not defensive.

Elizabeth had also been eager to enlist the help of the Dutch, and had offered to cancel their debts if they would contribute twenty-five ships. The response was enthusiastic and Jan van Duivenvoorde, Admiral of Holland and Lord of Warmond, a member of the Van Wassenaar family, noted for his great courage and fiery temper, was put in charge of preparations. The States-General agreed to pay him 400 florins a month (2,000 florins for the five months' voyage). As a young man he had been one of the aristocrats who led the *Guezen* [Sea Beggars], and as Admiral of the lakes of Haarlem and Leiden, helped to drive off the Spaniards besieging Leiden in 1576. One of his ancestral castles had been burnt down in this fighting. During the Armada campaign he had been in command at Dunkirk, where he was able to interrupt communications between the Duke of Parma's army and the Spanish fleet. His flagship was the *Neptune*; his Vice-Admiral, John Garbrandtsz of Enkuizen, sailed in the *Lion*; and his Rear-Admiral, Cornelis Leusen of Flushing, in the *Ele*. All these men attracted gentlemen-volunteers, among them Count Ludovic of Nassau and Van Duivenvoorde's kinsman, Jan van Doornik. The Admiralty of Holland contributed twelve men-of-war and four victuallers, the Admiralty of Zealand seven men-of-war and two victuallers. All sailed under the rebel tricolor with its horizontal orange, white and blue stripes, but Duivenvoorde, a member of the house of Orange-Nassau, particularly asked permission to fly the golden lion on a blue ground with a naked sword in one paw and seven arrows in the other, symbolising the seven northern provinces.[7]

Sir George, on his arrival in Dover, found the town in turmoil. Heavy gunfire could be heard from the direction of Calais.

'On Monday night [the 12th] the Earl of Essex came to Dover, where he found the Lord Admiral, who was in Dover Road, having with him the *Rainbow*, the *Vanguard*, the *Tremontana*, the *True Love*, the *Crane*, the *Answer*, the *Lion's Whelp*, the *Charles* and the *Moon*.

'On Tuesday the 13th April I came to Dover, where I found the Admiral [and] General honourably accompanied with many noblemen and gentlemen.

'On Wednesday the 14th there was nothing done but, as in the former days, sending and returning messengers to the French king, who attended our arrival at Boulogne. This day the citadel of Calais was won with a furious assault, the governor slain, and all the French put to the sword, but not as then known unto us.

'On Thursday the 15th. The French king's messenger, before day, came with letters from the king to the Earl of Essex, assuring him that the citadel would hold out some few days longer and desired him to hasten to meet him at St. John's Road, where he would attend his coming.'[8]

The French king, Henry IV, was at Boulogne, a day's march from Calais, and had sent urgent appeals for aid in a counter-attack. Since his succession to the throne seven years before, following the assassination of Henry III, he had recanted his Protestant heresies and been received into the Catholic Church. 'Three things are true,' he declared, 'but nobody believes them: that the Queen of England is a virgin; that I am a good Catholic; and that the Cardinal Archduke is a good general.' This was much too outspoken for Lord Burghley, who thought him ungrateful for the men, money and supplies that the Queen had provided in the past, and consequently the English commanders were doubtful what response to make to his appeal. The Privy Council feared that the King of Spain might dispatch a second Armada to the Channel and make Calais a port of embarkation from which the army in the Netherlands could invade England. Essex had made searching inquiries about this and come to the conclusion that, as no big ships could enter or leave the harbour except at high tide, there was no danger. Galleys might make Calais a base from which to harass English shipping, but being highly vulnerable when facing broadside firing, they were only effective in calm weather. For the Queen, to recapture a town that had been a valued possession of her Plantagenet, Lancastrian and Yorkist ancestors would be sweet but short-lived revenge. A man of Henry IV's temperament would insist that Calais be French, and she was therefore glad to answer his call for aid with the plea that her advisers would not permit her to comply.

'[15] The same morning likewise the Lords Generals received letters from Her Majesty giving them full authority and commission under the Great Seal to transport forces over for the recovery of Calais. Towards the evening there came to Dover 3,000 footmen divided into 3 regiments, viz: the Earl of Essex' Regiment, Sir Thomas Wellford's Regiment, and Sir Conyers Clifford's Regiment, which were presently embarked, and the same evening the Lords Generals, the great officers commanding and captains were all aboard ready to set sail, when at that instant a French gentleman from the Duke of Bouillon brought word of the loss of Calais, whereupon we returned to Dover.

'This day also the *Ark*, the *Mere Honour*, the *Lion*, the *Mary Rose*, the *Nonpareil*, and the *Swiftsure* came into Dover Road, and also Don Christophero, the king of Portugal's son, came out of France unto us.

'On Friday the 16th, early in the morning, the Duke of Bouillon,[9] Don Emanuel, the king of Portugal's eldest son, and Don Antonio Perez with 12 persons or thereabouts landed at Folkestone by Dover, whom the Earl of Essex with the lords and gentlemen brought into the town, within one house.[10]

'After his [Essex] arrival a fleet was discovered to the southward and the alarm taken that it was the Spanish fleet, whereupon in all possible haste the Lords Generals with the noblemen, captains, gentlemen and sonadians got aboard the ships, but in the end it proved to be Netherlanders and we returned to Dover.

'The same day the Duke of Bouillon, Don Emanuel and Antonio Perez rode towards the court. About supper time we had news that Sir Francis Vere with his troops [from the Netherlands] were at anchor before Boulogne.'[11]

The Duc de Bouillon had been given a most difficult mission. How could his master remove Spanish troops from French soil? Could the Portuguese princes Emanuel and Christopher be used in an attempt to subvert Spanish rule in Portugal? Antonio Perez, in the 1570's one of the most powerful men in Spain, being Secretary of State to Philip II and a renowned art collector, had been dismissed for treason, but was still regarded abroad as a possible source of useful intelligence. His appearance in the company of the Portuguese princes gave rise to rumours in Paris that either

Portugal or Biscay would be the English fleet's objective, suggestions reported by the Venetian ambassador to the Doge.[12] In fact they had not found any considerable support within Portugal or elsewhere and were little better than homeless refugees.

### Chapter I Notes

1. State Papers Domestic 1596.
2. The Archduke Albrecht was married to a daughter of Philip II; laymen were often appointed advisers to the Pope with the rank of Cardinal.
3. Lambeth Codex 250. The MS. begins in the first person, but quickly adopts the usage of the greatest general of antiquity, Julius Caesar, who always refers to himself in the third person. Perhaps Sir George, as page to the Earl of Leicester, a great patron of the New Learning, had heard men praise this literary device.
4. Birch, *Memoirs of the Reign of Queen Elizabeth*, Vol. I, London, 1754, quoting Cotton Library Otho ElX.
5. State Papers Domestic 1596. When, off the coast of Portugal, a general council was convened by displaying the red cross of St. George in the shrouds, the journal calls attention to it as 'a token'. This seems to indicate that it was a new signalling device.
6. Shakespeare, *King John* II i 67–71.
7. H. G. A. O'bree, *Geschiednis van hat geslacht van Wassenaar, 1200–1900*, Leiden, 1903.
8. Lambeth Codex 250.
9. Henry de la-Tour, Duc de Bouillon, a Huguenot and one of Henry IV's most trusted companions, was hereditary ruler of the princedom of Sedan on the borders of France and Luxembourg. A great medieval castle at Bouillon on the Semoy, a tributary of the Meuse, was his family seat. Sir George calls his followers 'sonadians'.
10. Philip II invaded and annexed Portugal in 1580. He had good grounds for claiming the throne, among them the fact that Princess Maria of Portugal had been his first wife. She died in giving birth to Don Carlos. The English supported the Pretender, Don Antonio, an illegitimate son of Sebastian, king of Portugal, whose death in battle in Africa led to Philip's succession. Don Antonio Perez had been one of Philip II's most trusted secretaries of state, but had turned traitor and stirred up an unsuccessful rebellion in Aragon.
11. Lambeth Codex 250.
12. State Papers Venetian 1596.

# II

# Our now
# set-out Army

To strengthen opinion at court in favour of continuing with the
original plan for the fleet and army, Sir George Carew wrote to Sir
Robert Cecil from *Mary Rose* about midnight on 16 April:

'This bearer, Mr.Bussby, needed no letter to spur me on to be
careful of him, for God is my witness, I am ready to entertain a
dog of yours that you esteem of with all the care I may . . . The
particulars of the loss of Calais, the Duke of Bouillon's coming to
the Court, fills your ears at large, as also of this day's alarm of the
Spanish fleet which proved nothing. Our generals make haste
away, wherein they have reason, for they burn daylight in Dover
Road. My Lord Thomas and Sir Walter Raleigh are not yet come
unto us with the remainder of the fleet; we hourly expect them,
but yet no cause of our stay, for they may follow in safety to
Plymouth. I think they will agree to be gone in the evening tide
tomorrow if watering do not cause them to stay, but Monday (if
not otherwise commanded) will be our longest abode here. This
evening tide Sir Francis Vere with his force came to an anchor
before Boulogne, where he attends farther directions. I do assure
you in my life I never saw more brave gentlemen assembled
together for any action than is now in Dover; had not Calais been
sooner lost than was feared, or was thought feasible in so short a
time, there is no doubt but we should have done our country
honour. Our ships are well and strongly manned, full of
munitions, and, as far as I can learn, plentifully victualled for the
time limited. If God be not against us, we need not care what
many may do unto us; and that which gives me good hope of
good success is the well-according of our generals, who yet, and I
hope will ever, run one course in their counsels.'[1]

In her most ornate and affectionate style Elizabeth wrote to the

25

Earl of Essex, claiming to have heard the Spanish guns in Greenwich:

> 'As distant as I am from your abode, yet my ears serve me too well to hear that terrible battery that me thinks sounds for relief at my hands; wherefore rather than for lack of timely aid it should be wholly lost, go you on, in God's Blessed Name, as far as that place where you may soonest relieve it, with as much caution as so great a trust requires. But I charge you, without the mere loss of it, do in no wise peril so fair an army for another Prince's town. God cover you under His safest wings, and let all peril go without your compass.'[2]

The Queen had decided not to devote ships or men to the recovery of Calais.

> 'On Saturday the 17th the 3 Regiments before mentioned were dismissed and letters were sent to Sir Christopher Blount, Sir John Wingfield and Sir Richard Wingfield to pay these regiments and to dissolve them: which regiments were levied in Essex, Sussex, Surrey and Middlesex.
>
> 'Towards the evening Sir Francis Vere with his fleet came into Dover Road. This day sundry merchants and hoys of our fleet came unto us from London.'[3]

When Sir Francis Vere arrived, Raleigh was still at Chatham, so that the question of their respective seniority did not arise until the end of May, when they met at Plymouth. After a quarrel, inflamed by drink, it was agreed that Raleigh should take precedence at sea and Vere on land.[4] Sir Walter, soldier, sailor, explorer, poet and once the most handsome man at court, had never learnt to control his temper, and the expedition was fortunate to have at hand Sir George, perhaps the only man capable of restraining him. Four years earlier, Raleigh had secretly married one of the ladies-in-waiting, and been confined to Durham House in the charge of Sir George. Mad to regain his freedom, he drew his dagger on his cousin, but Sir George and another friend overpowered him.

> 'On Sunday the 18th the Earl of Essex in the *Rainbow* set sail for Portsmouth, and Sir Francis Vere for Plymouth with his fleet.

The Lord Admiral by a pursuivant was sent for by the Queen to come to the court, who immediately posted thither. The Earl of Essex was likewise sent for, but the messenger came short of his being under sail before his coming. About sun-setting the wind came from the south south-west and blew a strong gale that we were enforced to weigh anchor and fall to the Downs.

'On Monday the 19th we rode all the day in the Downs, the Earl of Essex having contrary wind landed at Folkestone and from thence rode post to the court.'[5]

Those at court obviously had no conception of the difficulties and dangers caused by winds and tides to a mass of shipping lying at anchor in open water. Dover Road was exposed to the prevailing southwest winds, and so captains, forced to wait in the vicinity, took shelter behind the South Foreland in the quieter water off Deal known as the Downs, where they were also protected by the Goodwin Sands. Weighing anchor on the approach of rough weather was a laborious business. The sailors, pushing against the capstan bars, had to keep their feet on the heaving deck and avoid the beams above their heads. On the big ships there were two capstans, one abaft the mainmast and the other, called the jeer capstan, between the mainmast and the foremast, to heave upon the jeer rope. Such work needed strong, fit crews and they were hard to find, since scurvy was endemic, and often fatal, among the poor on land and on shipboard. Its cause, then unknown, was a deficiency in diet, and its first symptoms, often undetected, were weakness and lassitude. Sir Francis Drake had noticed, without understanding the reason, that the gentlemen who served under him were often physically stronger than the mariners, and declared: 'I must have the gentlemen haul and draw with the mariners and the mariners with the gentlemen.' Sir Richard, son of Sir John, Hawkins, had found oranges and lemons a preventative for scurvy, but, having been captured by the Spaniards in the Pacific and held in Panama, was unable to publish his discovery until many years later.[6]

In spite of the bad weather the promised contingent from the Netherlands got safely through the Straits.

'On Tuesday the 20th the *Vanguard* and the *Rainbow* set sail for

Plymouth to waft thither 600 sonadians of Ostend that were shipped in Flemish bottoms. This day 24 sail of Netherlanders that aid us in this voyage passed by us towards Plymouth. Divers of the Queen's lesser ships and of our merchant ships went with them. Also sundry ships this day of our fleet left in the Thames came unto us, whereof some of them stayed in the Downs with the Admiral and some other made for Plymouth.

'On Wednesday the 21st towards evening the *Nonpareil* and the *Lion's Whelp* put over to the coast of France to get intelligence of the enemy's designs touching his purpose for Boulogne.

'On Thursday the 22nd 2 ships of the North parts came to us to the Downs. They were coasters that were pressed for this voyage. All this night we had much wind.

'On Friday the 23rd, being St. George's Day, we weighed anchor and fell down into Dover Road.

'On Saturday the 24th the wind blew hard at south-west and south south-west which enforced the fleet to weigh anchor and fall into the Downs.

'On Sunday the 25th the ships remained in the Downs, and there tarried Monday the 26th day.

'On Tuesday 27th the ships came from the Downs back into Dover Road.

'On Wednesday the 28th in the morning a fleet of flyboats passing for Spain through the narrow seas were descried by our ships, whereupon they immediately weighed anchor and within three hours brought them into Dover Road, in all 10 sails. About noon the Lord Admiral came to Dover.

'On Thursday the 29th in the forenoon the Lord Admiral went aboard his ship. After dinner he dismissed 2 of the flyboats taken the day before; the other 8 he put captains and men into them sufficient to master the Dutches and so to attend his fleet. About two of the clock letters came by messenger of the chamber from Sir Robert Cecil to the Lord Admiral to will him in her Majesty's name to return to the court which once he purposed to have done, but upon better advice stayed. Towards night he caused proclamation to be made in Dover that all that were bound for this voyage should upon pain of death repair to their ships.

'After midnight on Friday morning the 30th the Lord Admiral shot off a piece and weighed anchor, whom all the fleet presently followed, holding our course westward. About noon athwart Pevensey Bay we met with a fleet of Netherlanders, in all 32 sail with whom the Admiral spake.

'On Saturday the 1st [of May] the wind for the most part was at south east and east south-east, the gale[7] very slender and an exceeding fair day.

'On Sunday the 2nd a little before day the wind began to blow hard at north-east and hawsie.[8] About seven of the clock much rain, at which time we entered into the Sound of Plymouth, where we came to an anchor. About 2 of the clock afternoon there was one in the *Mary Rose* ducked at the mainyard's arm.

'At our landing we found the Earl of Essex in Plymouth and all the great officers and captains of the Land Army where we attended the coming of the Rear Admiral with the remainder of the fleet, and in the meantime spent the days in training and sorting the companies into regiments.'[9]

Sir George Carew, as Master of the Ordnance, was responsible for supplying guns, ammunition, arms and armour to both the fleet and the army. He had Captain Goring for his second-in-command and Linewray as his clerk.[10] Military men, seeking to increase the mobility of their forces, were everywhere beginning to have doubts about the necessity of body armour, and the Master of the Ordnance had to meet a bewildering variety of demands. Halberdiers who guarded regimental colours preferred full-feathered high-combed helmets called morions, with the metal peaks curved upwards front and back to allow a better all-round view. Some wore a similar helmet without the comb, called a cabasset. A cuirass, which consisted of a breastplate and a backplate, was worn by musketeers and pikemen. In expensive armour the breastplate took the form of a peascod doublet, dipping low at the waist and having a ridge down the centre. A backplate that had been tested against pistol bullets was called 'a back at the proof'. As an alternative to the cuirass, jacks or brigandines, sleeveless tunics of heavy cloth or canvas with small sheets of metal sewn into them, were sometimes worn. For leg armour greaves to cover the shins were seldom used, and tasses for the thighs were made with light plates and sliding rivets. Not all the companies had muskets, some had the older arquebus or caliver, but several observers wrote admiringly of the arms drill and deportment of the men they saw at Plymouth.

The previous year the Queen had sent a fleet and an army under the joint command of Drake and Hawkins to attack the Spanish colonies in the Caribbean and New Spain. Essex, riding down to Plymouth to rejoin the fleet, encountered a messenger on his way to London with a report from Sir Thomas Baskerville, the commander of the land forces in the Caribbean. From him he learnt that both Hawkins and Drake were dead, and that Sir Thomas was approaching the Cornish coast with a mere remnant of their force, which had been repulsed at all points. Far from considering this bad news a reason for delay, Essex wrote to the Privy Council: 'Judge whether it is not time to draw our swords.'[11] Howard was no less eager to start; both commanders knew that in Spain *El Draque* had been the most feared of all Englishmen; there, a false sense of security would be a useful ally.

At court, talks with the Duc de Bouillon continued between 20 April and 16 May. While these were going on, the Queen sent to Howard and Essex in Plymouth a letter hinting that she might have to recall them and entrust their expedition to their deputies. This provoked just the response she desired, a unanimity among the commanders so strong that they put their hands to a joint letter of protest, endorsed in Cecil's handwriting: 'Sir G. Caru to me, a general letter', which read:

'It pleased the Lords Generals to acquaint us with a letter from her Majesty unto them touching their revocation in sort as is there expressed; wherein, because we are particularly interested by her Majesty's instructions, we have presumed to certify you of our opinions.

'First, if her Majesty do recall the Lords Generals, the reputation of the voyage (the advancement whereof is a special means to effect great designs) will be much blemished, for the opinion that is evermore held of the forces that are to serve under great commanders do terrify and discourage an enemy. Also, this army, being compounded of troops for sea and land service that have put themselves into this action, for the most part did enter into it out of particular love unto the Lords Generals, under whom they will be willing to serve and from others will withdraw themselves, not being possible for any other men to hold them together. This is not intended of the gentlemen voluntaries only, but of the whole troops, who, when they shall lose these great personages, will run away, whereby of necessity it follows that the army will be greatly diminished. And further, we doubt that the revocation of the Lords will be a cause of the diminution of the fleet, which if it follow, the like service cannot be effected which now we have hope of. And notwithstanding it is likely that divers of good quality in the army will continue the action, yet nevertheless, considering that such gentlemen be of great spirits, it is to be feared they will not be so well reduced to obey with willingness under commanders of less quality than the Lords Generals themselves; and what peril may grow in an army by mutinous spirits, this world hath too much experience. Another doubt, and that not the least of great importance, is to be made of the Netherland fleet, who, being drawn more willingly into this action than otherwise they would have been by the reputation of the commanders, may be discouraged, to the great hindrance of the action.

'Moreover, the rumour which hath possessed the world of these lords going in person with a mighty army, we may suppose hath so quickened the King of Spain's spirit as it is to be thought that he hath made all possible means of resistance throughout all the parts of his kingdom where it is likely that this fleet may or will approach, and strengthened the same to the uttermost. Which if he hath done, how perilous it will be to perform that which will be looked for, when the strength by land and sea shall be diminished, we leave to your wisdom.

'That the good hope, and almost without fear of ill-success (if God be not displeased with us), is likely to fall out if the Lords Generals be continued, we may easily judge, besides the particular knowledge we have of their worthiness, by the good agreement that is and doth remain betwixt them.

'Lastly, whereas it appears unto us that her Majesty's purpose

31

is to deject the carriage of her forces upon some persons that are now in the army, we do persuade ourselves that there is not any man willingly will undertake that charge, for the reasons before alleged.'[12]

With this emphatic advice from the army, Elizabeth reduced the aid promised to the French, sending only 2,000 men for four months, and allowed Howard and Essex to proceed.

The pre-Reformation custom of morning and evening prayers was to be continued and instructions to the fleet and army were read at service time. Captain John Smith, founder of Jamestown, Virginia, and almost certainly the Captain Smith who served in Sir Richard Wingfield's regiment, says:

> 'Give every mess a quarter can of beer and a basket of bread to stay their stomachs till the kettle be boiled, that they may first go to prayer, then to supper at six o'clock: sing a psalm, say a prayer, and the Master with his side begins the watch. Then all the rest may do what they will till midnight, and then his Mate with his larboard men with a psalm and a prayer relieves them till four in the morning. And so from eight to twelve each other.'[13]

No man was 'to dispute of matters of religion, as it is not fit that unlearned men should openly argue of so high and mystical matters'. Men infringing this regulation, or failing to report infringement, were to be 'banished the army'. Swearing, brawling, diceing and the like were forbidden 'as they breed contentions and discords'. Picking and stealing were to be severely punished.[14]

A special prayer for the success of the enterprise was received from the Queen with directions that it should be read on parade. This was probably composed by Burghley, who had studied the style of Archbishop Cranmer to considerable effect. After the Armada victory he had, with truly Erastian disregard for propriety, sent Archbishop Whitgift a thanksgiving prayer for use in churches. In 1596 he judged that the Queen's desire to be regarded as a lover of peace could conveniently be asserted in another prayer:

> 'Most omnipotent Maker and Guarder of all our world's mass, that only searchest and fathomest the bottom of all our hearts'

conceits, and in them seest the true original of all our actions intended; Thou that by thy foresight doest truly discern how no malice of revenge, nor quittance of injury, nor desire of bloodshed, nor greediness of lucre, hath bred the resolution of our now set-out Army, but a heedful care, a wary watch that no neglect of foes, nor oversurety of harm, might breed either danger to us or glory to them: These being grounds upon which Thou didst inspire the mind, we humbly beseech with bended knees, prosper the work, and with best forewinds guide the journey, speed the triumph of their fame, and surety to the realm, with the least loss of English blood. To these devout petitions Lord give thou thy blessed grant.'[15]

A sycophantic letter received by Anthony Bacon from a friend in Venice reported that an Italian translation of this prayer had been 'highly commended by all for true Christian devotion . . . as it was conceived in those parts that in England there was neither prayer, nor knowledge of Christ, nor indeed of religion.'[16]

It was a testing time for the Earl of Essex. On 12 May he wrote urgently to Cecil:

'If I seem unpatient, think how many things concur to move my patience. Sir Walter Raleigh, with the rest of our fleet, is not come and yet he hath (if the winds be the same there that they are here) all the wished winds he could desire, both to bring him out of the river and after he was in the Channel along to this place. Mr. Ashley is not come with our instructions, and yet I hear he was despatched long since. Mr. Dorrell is not [at] hand, who would help in bestowing the proportions of victual in every ship, and yet he promised to be here a week ago.

'I have not touched one penny of her Majesty's money, and have spent infinite sums of mine own, and neither here see any short end of my charge, nor find that above there is any feeling had of it. I pray you, therefore in friendship resolve me whether it be decreed by her Majesty that I only shall be undone and the service fall to the ground to the end that I with it might be ruined; for except her Majesty had given out some words to show her mislike or neglect of our going on, this slackness of all hands could not be used. I pay lendings to above 5,000 soldiers, I

33

maintain all the poor captains and their officers, I have a little world eating upon me in my house, am fain to relieve most of the captains and gentlemen and many soldiers that came from the Indies; and yet I complain not of charge, but of want of direction and certainty in your resolution above. Therefore, I do conjure you to deal freely with me in answering this letter, and to let me have answer quickly.'[17]

In the early stages of the preparations it had been agreed that Howard and Essex should pay a considerable amount towards the cost of the expedition out of their own pockets. On 11 January, 1596, Howard presented a statement to the Privy Council saying that he required two large sums: (a) £19,266 to victual 4,490 men serving in the Queen's ships for five months; of their wages, only enough would be paid out to cover 'coat and conduct money and rigging wages'[18]; the rest, £15,715, sea wages at 14s per man per month, would be held back until the expedition's return: (b) £21,400 for victuals for 5,000 foot soldiers at 6d a day. He would equip 1,000 men at his own expense, and pay off 2,000 after his return.[19] Soldiers were recruited for a campaign and cashiered at the end of it, like sailors at the end of a voyage, and, just as sailors had their pay reckoned by the day or month, but were paid in a lump sum, so were soldiers. They were entitled to 8d a day, but 6d of this was deducted for victuals, and the amount they received was 2d for every day's service.

The army was divided into nine regiments:

'*The Regiment of the Earl of Essex, Lord General*:
    Captain Aldridge, captain of my lord's horse:
    Captain Savage, 200 men;
    Sir Matthew Morgan, Lieutenant Colonel,
    Sir George Carew, Master of the Ordnance, and
    Captain Lambert, Quarter-Master-General, 150 men each;
    Captains Merkyrk, Sergeant Major,
    Sir Clement Heigham, Goring, and Hambridge, 100 men each.
'*The Regiment of the Lord Admiral, Lord General*:
    Captain Dutton, 200:
    Sir William Woodhouse, Lieutenant Colonel and

Captains Baynard, Sergeant Major,
Cottrell, Bacon, Digges, Gilbert, Waynman, Haynes,
Roberts and Gifford, 100 each.
'*The Regiment of Sir Francis Vere, Lord Marshal*:
Captain Dacres, 150:
Captains Bagnell, Heydon, Constable, Daniel Vere,
Upsher and Cary, 100 each.
'*The Earl of Sussex's Regiment*:
His own company, 150:
Captains Edward Conway, Fulk Conway, Wm. Harvey
Tyrrell, Wm. Williams and Rushe, 100 men.
'*Sir John Wingfield, Camp master his Regiment*:
His own company, 150:
Captains Horace Vere, Lawrence, Richard Mansfield,
Gerard Harvey, Charles Morgan and Ap Richard, 100 each.
'*Sir Conyers Clifford, Sergeant Major General, his Regiment*:[20]
His own company, 150:
Captains Merrick, Davyes, Pooley, Dauntsey,
Wilson, Talkerne, 100 each.
'*Sir Christopher Blount's Regiment*:
His own company, 150:
Captains Charles Blount, Brett, Thomas, Williams,
Harcourt, Folliett, Bolstred, 100 each.
'*Sir Richard Wingfield's Regiment*:
His own company, 150:
Captains Cuny, Jackson, Smith, Hopton, Fleming,
and Paulett, 100 each.
'*Sir Thomas Gerrard's Regiment*:
His own company, 150:
Captains Throgmorton, Floud, Billings, Collyer,
Salisbury and Molyneux, 100 each.'[21]

The colonels[22] served without pay, but were entitled to a major
part of the loot that their men might take, just as sea captains took
the lion's share of any prize their crew captured. Instructions
circulated by Essex at Plymouth, modelled on those in force under
Sir Francis Vere in the Netherlands, laid down that colonels were
to be in the vanguard in attack and in the rearguard in retreat; in

camp they were to pitch their tents in the midst of their men, and for drill they were to dismount and be at the right-hand end of the front rank.[23]

A captain was paid 6s a day, nearly nine times as much as a common soldier; he bought victuals in bulk and sold them at a profit. Estimate of the proportions of a soldier's daily victualling in August 1596 was:

> 'Flesh days:
>> Loaf of bread 1d
>> Pot of beer 1d
>> 1½ lbs of salt beef 2¼d
>
> Fish days
>> Bread and beer the same
>> Butter, cheese, or fish 2¼d
>
> The victualling of 2,000 men for four months will require
>> 933 qrs. of wheat; 633 tuns of beer; 480 hds of beef; 133 barrels of butter and 133 ways of cheese.'[24]

When supplies on this scale were available, the men were well fed. By modern standards the quantity is extraordinarily high.

The navy fared even better than the army, as the official 28-day ration scale for sailors shows:

> 'Fish days 10   Whereof 4 Fridays that have but 4 meals:
> Flesh days 16   so there wants 2 days.
> Fish days 20 meals.
> Flesh days 32 meals.
> The fare of fish days for every man per diem:
>> Biscuit 1 lb   Beer [½] gallon.
>> In fish 1 qr of stockfish, or the 8th part of a ling.
>> In cheese, per diem, 1 qr of a pound.
>> In butter, half qr per diem.
>
> The flesh day:
>> Beer and biscuit, *ut supra*.
>> Flesh, 2 lbs salt beef per diem, so as every man hath 1 lb for a meal, and 4 men have 4 lbs for a meal.
>
> For one day in the week:
>> A device for bacon for 1 day in a week.

1 lb of bacon for a man for a meal.

A pint of pease for 1 man for a meal.

I pottle of pease for 4 men.

4,000 cask will serve for 10,000 men for beer and beef for 3 months.

So there will be 3 days in the week—viz. Sunday, Tuesday and Thursday—for beef;

and 3 fish days—Wednesday, Friday and Saturday:

and Monday, for bacon and pease.'[25]

The men were divided into messes of four (as lawyers still are at Gray's Inn) and sometimes, to make the same victuals go further, into messes of six. On Fridays only half rations were to be issued, so that the saving on four Fridays amounted to whole rations for two days; so that the victuals for twenty-six days served for twenty-eight.

The expense of equipment was heavy; typical prices were a pike 2s.2d, a musket 20s, a caliver 15s, 1 lb of corned gunpowder 1s and 100 lb of match 20s.[26] Orders for powder and shot were sent to the Master of Ordnance by captains, and his clerk issued the required quantities in return for a receipt, presented on pay day to the Treasurer or Auditor, who stopped the amount from the money due to the captain and his men.[27] Sir George was to keep two books, one for the army and one for the navy.[28]

Each captain had, as his second-in-command, a lieutenant, paid 3s a day; an ensign-bearer, a man of gentle birth, attended by an ensign guard of halberdiers; two sergeants, each with three corporals, who were responsible for drill, equipment and the issue of victuals; and two drummers, who summoned the men to assemble, beat time on the march, and, by a recognised series of drum-beats, gave battle orders that could be heard above the noise of firearms and the cries of the wounded.

Ensigns, sergeants and drummers were paid 1s.6d a day. There was usually a ratio of two pikemen to every musketeer, and service with the pike was held to be the more honourable.

Captains were often accused of drawing the pay of dead men or deserters whose names were on the muster book, but not answered

37

to. These 'dead pays' were also called 'faggots' or 'shadows'. John Donne, who saw the army in training, did not forget the practice:

'First swear by thy best love in earnest
(If thou which lovest all, can love any best)
Thou wilt not leave me in the middle street,
Though some more spruce companion thou dost meet,
Not though a Captain do come in thy way
Bright parcel gilt, with forty dead men's pay.'[29]

Raleigh was no less ardent than Essex and Howard, and the expedition appealed to everything in his restless and ambitious nature. The year before he had returned from a voyage to Guiana, where he dreamt of winning for the Queen an American empire richer than any yet discovered. Delay might give the Spaniards time to make ready their defences. Now Elizabeth agreed that the best answer to the long-sustained hostility of Philip II was a major attack. Long afterwards, Raleigh criticised her failure to hold consistently to this opinion:

'If the late Queen would have believed her men of war as she did her scribes, we had in her time beaten that great empire to pieces and made their kings kings of figs and oranges, as in old times.'[30]

On 4 May, still delayed in Kent, rounding up the remainder of the ships and their crews, he wrote to Cecil:

'I cannot write to our Generals at this time, for the pursuivant found me in a country village, a mile from Gravesend, hunting after runaway mariners, and dragging in the mire from ale-house to ale-house; and could get no paper but that the pursuivant had this piece. Sir, by the living God, there is no King nor Queen nor General nor any else can take more care than I to be gone.'[31]

Continuing bad weather brought, on 12 May, near-disaster to his squadron:

'Since I sent my letter to your Honour from Dover before I departed the Road, there came up unto view some seven or eight sail of the fleet, who being all like to perish on Wednesday, after midnight they were driven to let slip all their cables and anchors.

I humbly beseech your Honour to cause a letter to be written to the mayor of Dover to send a boat of the town's to save the said cables and anchors, having all buoys upon them. They were let on the north-east part of Goodwin Sands in five or six fathoms.'[32]

But at last

'On Friday the 21st about 7 of the clock in the morning the Rear Admiral came to an anchor in the Sound of Plymouth with the residue of the fleet, after whose arrival the time was industriously spent in revictualling the fleet and supplying of all the other defects insomuchas on the last of May all the land companies and the whole army were shipped and the greatest part of the ships that were in Cattwater warped out into the Sound.'[33]

Sir George's young Commissary-General of Munitions, Captain (later Sir William) Slingsby of Knaresborough, Yorkshire, afterwards compiled a list of the ships in each squadron:

'*The Lord Admiral's Squadron*
 Of the Queen's ships
The Lord Admiral, in the *Ark Royal*, Admiral of the Fleet and of
 this squadron
Sir Robert Southwell, in the *Lion*, Vice-Admiral of this
 squadron
Captain Alexander Clifford, in the *Dreadnought*, Rear Admiral
Captain Richard Leveson in the *True Love*
[Captain William King] in the *Lion's Whelp*, a pinnace
 Of the Merchant ships
*The Swan*
The hoy of Sandwich
*The Darling*
*The Delight*
*The Desire*
*The Expedition*
*The Elizabeth* of Hampton
*The Pleasure* of Bristol
*The Elizabeth Jonas* of Hull
*The Unicorn* of Bristol

*The Corbett* of Ipswich
*The Elizabeth* of London
*The Prudence* of Plymouth
*The Jacob* of Enkuizen
*The Mermaid* of Dartmouth
The great ship of Flushing
*The Yager* of Schiedam
With 5 sail of hoys and flyboats laden with horses and private
  provision.

In all 28 sail

'*The Earl of Essex his Squadron*
  Of the Queen's ships
The Earl of Essex, in the *Due Repulse*, Admiral also of the Fleet
  and of this squadron
Sir Francis Vere, in the *Rainbow*, Vice-Admiral
Sir John Wingfield, in the *Vanguard*, Rear Admiral
The Prince of Portugal, in the *Tremontana*
[Captain Sackville Trevor] in the *Charles*, a pinnace
  Of the Merchant ships
*The Lioness*
*The Mynion*
*The Jonathan*
*The Cherubim*
*The Brave*
*The Gift of God*
*The Marygold*
*The Chameleon*
*The Posthorse*
*The Howard*
The bark Rowe
*The Green Dragon*
*The Phoenix* of Amsterdam
*The Swan*
The great ship of Flushing
*The Mermaid*
With 5 sail of hoys and flyboats laden with horses and private
  provisions.

In all 28 sail

'*The Lord Thomas Howard's squadron*
  Of the Queen's ships
The Lord Thomas Howard,[34] in the *Merhonour*, Vice-Admiral of
  the Fleet and Admiral of this squadron
Captain Robert Dudley,[35] in the *Nonpareil*, Vice-Admiral
Captain Robert Mansell, in the *Crane*, Rear Admiral
Captain Henry Moyle, in the *Moon*, a pinnace
  Of the Merchant ships
*The Hunter* of Schiedam
*The Violet* of London
*The Golden Dragon*
*The Grace of God*
*The Exchange*
*The Ruben*
*The Hunter* of Enkuizen
*The Joshua* of Hamburg
*The Hercules* of Rye
*The Brown Fish*
*The Roger and Katherine*
*The Endeavour*
*The Jonas*
*The Alcedo*
*The George*
*The Jacob* of Rotterdam
*The Mary Margaret*
With 4 hoys and flyboats laden with horses and private
  provisions.
In all 25 sail.

'*Sir Walter Raleigh's squadron*
  Of the Queen's ships
Sir Walter Raleigh, in the *Warspite*, Rear Admiral of the Fleet
  and Admiral of this squadron
Sir George Carew, in the *Mary Rose*
Captain Robert Crosse, in the *Swiftsure*, Vice-Admiral
Captain George Gifford, in the *Quittance*, Rear Admiral
  Of the Merchant ships
*The Roebuck*
*The Centurion*

*The Primrose*
*The Great Katherine*
*The Experience*
*The Mary Anne*
*The Peter* of London
*The Jacob* of Akersloot
*The St. Peter* of Enkuizen
*The Blue Pigeon*
*The Prudence*
*The Amulo*
*The Popinjaye*
*The Jacob* of Enkuizen
The new Flemish hulk
With 4 hoys and flyboats laden with horse and provisions.

In all 23 sail

'*The Flemish Squadron*
    Of the Flemish Ships of War
John [van] Duivenvoorde, Admiral of Holland and Lord of
    Warmont, in the *Neptune*, Admiral of this squadron
Captain John Gerbrantsen of Enkuizen, in the *Lion*, Vice-
    Admiral
Captain Cornelius Leusen of Flushing, in the *Ele*, Rear Admiral
With 15 sail more of men-of-war and 6 hoys and flyboats laden
    with munition and victuals for supply.

In all 24 sail

'*In these Five Squadrons*
    Of the Queen's ships and pinnaces   18
    Of merchant ships                   68
    Of hoys and flyboats                18
    Of the Flemish squadron             24
In all the fleet 128 sail
Besides great store of ships and barks from divers parts that
followed the fleet upon their own adventures for purchase and
pillage.'[36]

This list shows how small a proportion of the whole fleet the
Queen's ships were. Being three-masted vessels of the galleon type
with high castles fore and aft, they were difficult to handle in

variable winds. On the fore and main masts the large square-rigged sails, if filled by a following wind, gave a maximum speed of about six knots, which was good enough in a chase, but to aid the helmsman the mizzen mast was fitted with a lateen sail, copied from Mediterranean craft. In the bows a massive bowsprit supported a small square sail worked from a stout platform, known as a beakhead. Armament varied considerably between ship and ship. *Mary Rose*, 600 tons, had 39 guns (four 34-pounders; eleven 18-pounders, ten 14-pounders, and fourteen lighter pieces). By comparison *Ark Royal* (formerly *Ark Raleigh*) 694 tons, the Admiral's flagship, was, for her tonnage, more heavily armed, having 55 pieces, including four 30-pounders, twelve 9-pounders, twelve 8-pounders, six 6-pounders and seventeen light guns. She was built in 1587 for Sir Walter Raleigh, and Captain John Smith described her proportions as 'the best because the counterpoise on each side doth make her swim perpendicular or straight and consequently steady which is the best'.[37] She was sold to the Queen, re-named *Ark Royal*, and allotted to Howard for the Armada campaign. The Admiral, writing to Lord Burghley, was enthusiastic about her quality:

'I pray you tell her Majesty from me that her money was well given for the *Ark Raleigh*, for I think her the odd ship in the world for all conditions; and truly I think there can be no sail great or small, but how far soever they be off, we fetch them and speak with them.'[38]

Two new galleons, *Due Repulse* and *Warspite*, had been completed in record time and Howard wrote with pride to Sir Robert Cecil on 7 March:

'My lord Thomas [Howard], Sir W. Raleigh and myself were yesterday from eight in the morning till three in the afternoon very busy at Mr. Quarles'[39] office, and after, till it was night, Sir Walter and myself were up and down on the river continually busied. If you were but one day with us, you should see whether we have any spare time. . . . I promised Her Majesty the two new ships should be builded by the 20 March; it was performed before, and yet everybody said it was impossible, but I assure you my often eye and my purse was the furtherer of it.'[40]

43

The measurements of the new ships were

|  | Keel | Beam | Depth | Burden | Tonnage* |
|---|---|---|---|---|---|
| Due Repulse | 105 | 37 | 16 | 622 | 777 |
| Warspite | 90 | 36 | 16 | 518 | 648 |

\* See Appendix III.

The most effective ratio between beam and keel was at the time, as for long after, a matter of argument among shipwrights. In these new ships it was nearly 3 to 1, the ratio given for a galleon by William Borough, Controller of the Admiralty at this time, and regarded by younger men as an improvement on the older 2½ to 1 ratio. Due Repulse had 48 guns (total weight about 67 tons) and Warspite 40 (about 52 tons). The type of gun most favoured throughout the fleet was the demi-culverin. Carew had written to Cecil in 1594 that in the sea service demi-culverin were 9 feet long compared with the normal 12 feet.[41] By 1596 they were even shorter, 16 out of 20 supplied to Due Repulse and 8 out of 12 for Warspite being only 8½ feet. These fired a 9 lb shot and, being so much shorter than the demi-culverin used on land, could be more easily swabbed out and re-charged.

Many of the merchant ships matched the Queen's ships in size and armament. They were sent to sea as privateers on a joint-stock principle, the proceeds from captures being divided, after a deduction of one tenth for the Lord High Admiral, into thirds, one for the owners, one for the victuallers and one for the officers and men.

Normally, an expedition of this size would have required a Treasurer of the Army (Treasurer at War), but Her Majesty had by her commission 'given power unto Sir George Carew, Master of the Ordnance, Mr. Antony Ashley, Secretary, and Mr. Marmaduke Dorrell, the Victualler-General, to take into their charge (with the privity of the Lords Generals) to her use such purchase and prizes of value as should be taken'.[42] Unnecessary risks in pursuit of profit or glory were to be avoided. The slaughter of women, children or the aged was prohibited. A code of conduct was issued to the whole fleet. No man, on pain of death, was to land in any country without orders, nor go to another ship without his captain's leave. At sea the soldiers must help the mariners when ordered to do so. No man whatsoever was to strike the captain, lieutenant, master or other officer, on pain of death.

To avoid the risk of fire no man, on pain of severe punishment, was to use a candle without a lanthorn. Fire at sea was one of the most dreaded of disasters, and Howard ordered that boats were to be sent to any ship in danger. Gunpowder was to be carefully preserved from spoil and waste, as 'without it there can be no great service'. Ships were not 'to carry too high sail when going by the wind, and especially in a high sea, as the spoil of the masts must endanger the enterprise'. Disabled ships were to signal the rest of the fleet:

'If a ship happen to spring a mast, to fall into a leak, or such mischance, which God forbid, a piece shall be shot off, or if it be night, two pieces and bear two great lights, one a man's height and a half above another.'

The squadrons were 'to keep good breadth' from each other and either the Admiral or the Rear Admiral was always to be in the rear. Directions for the avoidance of collisions were precise:

'In fogs, if any happen, when your ships are becalmed, you shall cause some noise to be made by drum, by trumpet, by shooting of a musket, or caliver now and then, or by some like means that, by hearing you to be near, one may take heed lest he fall foul of another.'[43]

At night the look-out men watched the lights of the ships around them, ready to give warning if any came too close. Sometimes this duty was given, as Shakespeare knew, to mere boys:

'Wilt thou [Sleep] upon the high and giddy mast
Seal up the ship-boy's eyes and rock his brains
In cradle of the rude imperious surge,
And in the visitation of the winds,
Who take the ruffian billows by the top,
Curling their monstrous heads, and hanging them
With deafening clamour in the slippery clouds,
That, with the hurly, death itself awakes?
Canst thou, O partial Sleep! give thy repose
To the wet sea-boy in an hour so rude?'[44]

45

Each squadron was instructed to keep together and 'not to chase any ship without orders'. A white pennant flown by the Admiral indicated that a chase could be started by one ship; two white pennants for two ships; and three for three. If a prize were taken, no spoil was to be removed from it, and account was to be rendered for everything on board. If any ship encountered one of the King of Spain's ships, she was to go to the Admiral for instructions.[45]

Elaborate precautions were taken against the possibility that neutral countries, finding their traditional overseas trade violently disrupted by the operations of Howard and Essex, might claim compensation. A 'declaration' therefore, drafted by Burghley, but made in their names, was published on the continent in French, Italian, Dutch and Spanish and 'distributed into as many ports of Spain and Portugal as conveniently might be'. It ran as follows:

'To all Christian people to whom this declaration shall come to be read or heard, greeting . . . We do give all men knowledge that this said navy under our charge is by Her Majesty prepared and sent to serve on the seas for the defence of Her Majesty's realm, dominions and subjects against such mighty forces as we are advised from all parts of Christendom to be already prepared by the King of Spain, and by further provision of men and ships, daily sent for, are to be mightily increased to invade Her Majesty's realm, as heretofore in the year of our Lord 1588 was attempted . . . And because Her Majesty hath good intelligence of perfect amity with all kings and princes of Christendom, saving only with the King of Spain, who hath these many years most unjustly professed openly great inimity by divers actions, both against her royal person and her countries and people, without any just cause first given on Her Majesty's part; therefore we, the said Earl and Lord Admiral, do ascertain all persons that we are most strictly commanded by Her Majesty to forbear from offending in this our voyage in any manner persons of what nation soever except the said King's natural subjects, or such other born strangers as shall give to the said King manifest aid with men, ships, artillery, victuals or other warlike provisions for invasion of Her Majesty. And do therefore give strait charge to all persons that shall serve in this navy underneath us, upon pain of extreme punishment, to observe the same. Yet, to avoid all occasions that may breed question . . . we do earnestly and in God's name require and charge all persons that are not the said King's natural subjects and yet have given him aid . . . to withdraw all their said ships prepared for war . . . and therewith to return, either to their own countries or, if they shall so like, to come to our navy. And, if any . . . shall not endeavour themselves to perfect this reasonable request, we shall then be justly moved, as by the law of arms we may, to take and use all such for refusing this our offer as manifest aiders of the King of Spain . . . And if any harm shall happen by any attempts . . . of our navy there shall be no just cause for them hereafter to complain, or to procure their natural princes and lords to solicit restitution.'[46]

Behind all this verbiage the commanders observed with gratitude that, whatever ships they captured during their voyage, the Queen would, without regard to their country of origin, allow them to be lawful prizes.

Each evening every ship was to come as near as she could to speak to the Admiral, who was to do the same to the General.[47] This ceremony of 'hailing', called in modern times 'manning ship' and 'three cheers', was vividly described by Dr. Roger Marbecke, who at sixty had never been to sea before and so was fascinated by many things that the sailors took for granted:

'When after a day's absence or more, they come near to the Lord Admiral, and yet not too near, but of such a reasonable distance as they may not endanger themselves of going foul one of another, they presently man the ship and place every one of their companies both upon the upper and middle deck and also upon the waist and shrouds and elsewhere to the most advantage they can make the bravest show and appear the greatest number. Then the masters and mates of the ships immediately [join] upon the sounding of their whistles in a pretty loud tunable manner, all the whole company shaking their hands, hats and caps, giving a marvellous loud shout, consisting of so many loud, strong and variable voices maketh such a sounding echo and pleasant report in the air, as delighteth very much. And this ceremony is done three times by them, and three times interchangeably answered.'[48]

A letter from the Queen, in the form of a prayer, reached Essex in Plymouth at the end of May:

'I make this humble bill of requests to Him that all makes and does, that with His benign Hand He will shadow you so, as all harm may light beside you, and all that may be best, hap to your share; that your return may make you better, and me gladder. Let your companion, my most faithful Charles, be sure that his name is not left out in this petition. God bless you both.'[49]

This prompted him to dictate a memorandum addressed to the Privy Council, which he called a 'meditation'. It began with a modest disclaimer of any personal responsibility for the project of attacking Spain, but went on to describe the advantages that would ensue if a port were not only captured, but garrisoned and held so that it became 'a thorn sticking in the King of Spain's foot'. Knowing how much the Queen disliked spending money, he continued:

'The objections against this will be hazard, and charge; hazard to hold anything of so mighty a King's, and charge to send such supplies as will be needful; but it is not the hazard of a State or the whole,—as are the hazards of a defensive war,—but only a hazard of some few, and such commanders as shall be set out for such a service; those also that shall be so hazarded shall be in less danger than if they were put into any frontier places of France or of the Low Countries, for they should not be left in any part of the continent of Spain or Portugal where the enemy might bring army upon army to attempt them, (though I doubt not but after he had once tried what it was to besiege 2,000 or 3,000 English in a place well fortified, and where they had a port open, he would grow quickly weary of those attempts), but they should be so lodged that the state and strength of the place should warrant their safety; so that to pull Her Majesty's men out of it should be a harder task than to conquer any country that flanks upon the firm land by him, [marginal note in Cecil's hand reads "Give the name"] and to let the English quietly possess it should so much

48

1. George Carew, Kt 1586; Baron Clopton 1605;
Privy Councillor 1616; 1st Earl of Totnes 1626.
Master of Ordnance and commander of the *Mary Rose*.
(*National Portrait Gallery, London*)

2. Page from the *Mary Rose* Journal for 21 June 1596
recording the naval fight and the landing at Cadiz.
(*Lambeth Palace Library*)

4. Robert Devereux, 2nd Earl of Essex,
on horseback, by R. Boissard.
(*Crown copyright Victoria & Albert Museum*)

3. Charles, Lord Howard of Effingham, on horseback with
pictures of the Armada and Cadiz actions inset.
(*Reproduced by courtesy of the
Trustees of the British Museum*)

5. Sir Francis Vere, commander of the land forces. (*From a private collection. Photo: National Portrait Gallery, London*)

6. John Donne, gentleman volunteer, poet, and later Dean of St Paul's. (*National Portrait Gallery, London*)

prejudice him as he were not able to endure it. And for charge, there needs not so much be expended but that it might easily be borne, and the place being well chosen, and the war well conducted, in a short time there would not only arise enough to pay the charge, but greater profit to Her Majesty, and wealth to our country would grow from the place that should be held; for in a short time, a great part of the golden Indian stream might be turned from Spain to England, and Her Majesty be made able to give law to all the world by sea, without her charge. . . . [in Essex's own hand] I beseech you to pardon my using another hand for this transcript, as I have been forced to go from ship to ship to make our loiterers go out of harbour, and made my hand unable to write so long a letter.'[50]

To Sir George Carew the might of Spain was no less formidable than it appeared to Essex, yet he wrote to Sir Robert Cecil on 21 May much more confidently:

'I do not know that man that I am so much bound unto as unto your honour, and therefore I were a damned villain if I did not love you most . . . I do not know how time may alter in foreign parts the disposition of great commanders; hitherto I do find myself exceedingly well dealt with withal, and nothing in their governments but that which deserves all praise and honour . . . [Our forces are] strong enough to abide the proudest fleet that ever swam, and by land our army, both in numbers and gallant men, is of strength sufficient to march and retreat in safety from a more puissant enemy that we are like to find; for in his own country, by the wisest, he is held to be weakest.'[51]

### Chapter II Notes

1. Hatfield 40.10.
2. W. C. Devereux, *Lives and Letters of the Devereux Earls of Essex*, London, 1853.
3. Lambeth Codex 250.
4. Birch, *Commentaries of Sir Francis Vere*, Cambridge, 1637.
5. Lambeth Codex 250.
6. *The Observations of Sir Richard Hawkins on his voyage into the South Sea AD 1593*, London, 1622.
7. The word gale was applied to any wind, not, as now, only to a strong one.

8. Hawsie—possibly a wind that caused the ship to pitch and take in water through the hawse holes, through which the anchor cables pass.
9. Lambeth Codex 250.
10. State Papers Domestic 1596. Linewray became Surveyor of Ordnance in 1602. In that year Sir George Carew invented a cannon that could be taken to pieces for easy conveyance, repair and construction (see H. L. Blackmore, *The Armouries of the Tower of London*, HMSO, 1977).
11. W. C. Devereux, *Lives and Letters of the Devereux Earls of Essex*, London 1853.
12. Hatfield 40.100.
13. Captain John Smith, *A Sea Grammar*, London, 1627.
14. State Papers Domestic 1596. All these offences were mentioned as likely to occur among the men serving in the Spanish Armada, and were specifically forbidden in Philip II's instructions to his commanders.
15. Lambeth Codex 250.
16. Birch, *Memoirs of the Reign of Queen Elizabeth*, Vol. II, London, 1754.
17. Hatfield 40.75. Those 'from the Indies' were Baskerville's force.
18. The coat was a white overall with the red cross of St. George on the chest, and the conduct money was travel expenses for the journey to the point of assembly, in this case Plymouth.
19. State Papers Domestic 1596.
20. Sir Conyers Clifford, member of Parliament for Pembroke, had been knighted during the siege of Rouen, where he rescued the body of Essex's brother Walter from the enemy.
21. Hatfield 47.94.
22. Colonel: From Italian *Colonello*, a little column. So called because he led the 'little column' at the head of the regiment.

    Major: A 'greater' or more important than the company officers. The lowest rank of field officer.

    Captain:: From French *Capitaine*. Simply 'the head' of a company or small unit. A very similar rank to that of the Roman centurion, or commander of a hundred.

    Lieutenant: French, 'one who acts as a substitute' for a captain, colonel, general, etc.

    Ensign: From French *Enseigne*. The junior commissioned rank of infantry. Named from the ensign or colour, which he carried.

    Cornet: Equivalent of Ensign in the regiments of horse. Named from the cornet (standard or guidon).
23. State Papers Domestic 1596.

24. State Papers Domestic 1596.
25. State Papers Domestic 1588.
26. G. Cruickshank, *Elizabeth's Army*, Oxford University Press, 1966.
27. Thomas Digges, *Four Paradoxes, or Politique Discourses concerning Military Discipline*, 1604.
28. State Papers Domestic 1596.
29. John Donne, *Satire I*.
30. Sir Walter Raleigh, *The History of the World*.
31. Hatfield 40.60.
32. Hatfield 173.73.
33. Lambeth Codex 250.
34. Lord Thomas Howard, son of the fourth duke of Norfolk by his second marriage, was distantly related to Charles, Lord Howard of Effingham. Both were able fleet commanders, and respected one another's professional ability.
35. Robert Dudley, born 7 August 1574, an illegitimate son of the Queen's favourite, the Earl of Leicester, by Lady Douglas Sheffield, had explored the coast of Guiana. A great expert on seafaring and naval affairs, he later entered the service of the Grand Duke of Tuscany, and had a palazzo in Florence. Author of *Arcano del Mare*, 1646.
36. Duke of Northumberland's MS. Slingsby gives the number of merchant ships in the Admiral's squadron as 18, but only lists 17. The missing name may be *Affection*, 120 tons, known to have been with the fleet. She, like the great *Alcedo*, 400 tons, was owned by Sir John Watts, a leading London merchant. The designation 'Great Ship of Flushing' may occur twice because no note had been made of individual Dutch names.
37. Captain John Smith, *A Sea Grammar*, London, 1627.
38. State Papers Domestic 1588.
39. Mr. Quarles was a surveyor of the navy victuals.
40. Hatfield 30.106.
41. State Papers Domestic 1594.
42. Duke of Northumberland's MS.
43. State Papers Domestic 1596.
44. Shakespeare, *Henry IV Part II* III i 18–27.
45. State Papers Domestic 1596.
46. State Papers Domestic 1596.
47. State Papers Domestic 1596.
48. Rawlinson D124.
49. W. C. Devereux, *Lives and Letters of the Devereux Earls of Essex*, London, 1853.
50. State Papers Domestic 1596.
51. Hatfield 41.32.

# III

# What
# enterprise was fittest

'On Tuesday the 1st [of June] about four a clock in the morning the Admiral Howard shot off a warning piece to give knowledge to the fleet of his departure and about 7 of the clock, the wind being at west north-west, set sail and put forth to the sea, after whom did follow a good part of the fleet confusedly, and at 12 a clock the Vice-Admiral set sail. Towards night the Admiral Essex, the Admiral of Holland and the Rear Admiral with all the rest of the fleet put to the sea, all which day and night following the wind holding shift at west north-west we plied off and on between the Rame Head and Fowey.

'2. On Wednesday morning we found ourselves athwart of Fowey not above 3 leagues[1] from the shore, the wind as before. All which day we plied up and down till, towards four a clock, at which time, finding the wind south-west, the Admiral Howard came room[2] for the Sound of Plymouth, after whom the fleet followed, and before eight a clock were all at anchor, part in the Sound and part at Cawshant Bay: and immediately the Generals gave commandment upon pain of death that no man should go ashore; which done, the Selected Council, together with the Admiral, Vice-Admiral and Rear Admiral of Holland, met aboard the Admiral Howard. To resolve what enterprise was fittest to be undertaken for the annoyance of the Spanish king, where it was concluded by the general opinion of the Council, and with the assent of the Lords Generals, that Cadiz in south Spain was fittest to be attempted as a place of importance to impeach the enemy, most easy to [be] surprised, and in itself rich, besides the good possibility to sack Port Real, Port Santa Maria, St. Lucar and Xeres, as also to burn and take such ships and galleys as should be found in the places aforesaid.

'It was also resolved that no part of Spain should in any case be approached or attempted by any of our fleet, nor, if we could otherways choose, come within sight of the Spanish coast until we come to the height of Cape St. Vincent, commonly called the southwardly cape, and further, if it should so happen that by foul weather our fleet should be severed, it was there likewise decreed that all the ships should make their rendezvous at Cape St. Vincent, and those that should fortune first to make the Cape should lie off, not within sight of the land, until some one of the Admirals of the Squadrons were come up from whom they were to receive directions and to attend that said Admiral till the whole fleet were united; and that every sea captain might have notice hereof it was likewise thought good that the said captains should generally have a billet, sealed up with the Lords Generals' seals, wherein should be set down these resolved directions, with commandment, upon pain of death not to break open the same until they should be by such extremity enforced thereto. Which said directions were set down in these words and dispersed at sea with all possible expedition:—

'Whereas it may happen (as often is experienced) that some of the fleet may by foul weather or otherways lose the company of his squadron of the fleet, for the better prevention of the great inconveniences usually thereby following, we do hereby straitly will and command all captains and masters of every such ship as shall by any occasion so lose company that they fail not to shape and direct their course to the height of the Cape St. Vincent, otherways called the South Cape of Spain, making only the land thereof, and not to come so near as to be discovered from it by the enemy, where a couple of pinnaces or some other meet vessels shall purposely attend for their further direction. And if they shall not find any vessel there to this purpose, then shall they make off and on there in the height of that Cape till some Admiral of a Squadron shall come whose direction they shall obey for their further repair, whereof you may not fail at your uttermost perils.

Aboard the *Due Repulse* in Cawshant Bay the second of June 1596

Essex    C. Howard

'Poster:

Howbeit our meaning is, if you find us not at the Cape, that you come immediately for Cadiz in Andalusia.

'The direction on the back side [of] the billet sealed up—as followeth—and delivered to every ship in haec verba If you be separated from the fleet by foul weather or otherways, you shall herein find to what place you shall repair, till when you shall not open the enclosed upon pain of death.'[3]

It would have been impossible to reach, at this one meeting of the Council of War, the decision to attack Cadiz and to have had so many 'billets' prepared for delivery, unless Howard, Essex and a few senior commanders had privately agreed on their destination many months earlier.

'3. On Thursday morning the Lord Admiral Howard went in his barge to Plymouth to press forth the [space left blank] in place of the *Jonas*, wherein Master Fyshborne was captain and Captain Collyer's company transported, for that the day before, whilst we were at sea, the ship being old, leaks did grow so fast upon her as with great travail she was kept from sinking, and about ten of the clock the Lord Admiral Howard, with his squadron following him, set sail to sea again, the wind being at north-west, and after him the other Admirals with their squadrons followed, so as the Rear Admiral with the last of the fleet were by four a clock under sail.

'4.5. On Friday and Saturday the wind continued for the most part at west north-west, and north-west, with some calms.

'6. On Sunday morning about an hour and [a] half before day, the weather being foul, and a port gale of wind at the north-west, the *Mary Rose* spent her main yard, whereupon (to give warning of that mischance to the fleet) she shot off 2 pieces and in the shrouds did hang out two lights a man's height one above another, at which signs the Rear Admiral with many other ships came room unto her to understand what distress she was in and to give her help, but, thanks be to God, the breaking of the main yard was all the hurt she received, after in a few days repaired. All this day the wind continued still (but dry) at the north-west,

with a stiff gale, and a grown sea. About noon we found
ourselves in 48 degrees and odd minutes.'[4]

The general terror and damage to the ship is vividly recalled by
John Donne:

'Sooner than you read this line did the gale,
Like shot, not fear'd till felt, our sails assail . . .
Some coffin'd in their cabins lie, equally
Griev'd that they are not dead, and yet must die;
And as sin-burd'ned souls from graves will creep,
At the last day, some forth their cabins peep:
And trembling ask what news, and do hear so,
Like jealous husbands, what they would not know.
Some sitting on hatches, would seem there,
With hideous gazing to fear away fear.
Then note they the ship's sicknesses, the Mast
Shaked with this ague, and the Hold and Waist
With a salt dropsy clog'd, and all our tacklings
Snapping, like too-high-stretched treble strings.
And from our tottered sails rags drop down so,
As from one hang'd in chains, a year ago.
Even our Ordinance plac'd for our defence,
Strive to break loose and scape away from thence.
Pumping hath tir'd our men, and what's the gain?
Seas into seas thrown, we suck in again.'[5]

One of the terrors of every voyage was the possibility that in
rough seas one of the cannon on its carriage and wheels of wood
might break loose, and, with a rolling of the ship, run back and
forth, crushing and smashing all in its way, a monster defiant of
every attempt to cage it.

'7. 8. Monday and Tuesday fair weather, the wind being as
before.
'9. Wednesday all the fore part of the day calm. Towards
evening stormy with a stiff gale at the north-west and some rain
wherewith the *Swiftsure* spent her fore mast, whereupon the
Lords Generals with the whole fleet tacked about and made in

with her, but, thanks be to God, there was no man hurt, and the next day the mast fished.'[6]

Concerning the *Swiftsure*, Sir George first wrote 'the mast made serviceable', but crossed this out and put 'fished', the proper nautical term for putting a fractured mast in splints. Though a gunner, not a sailor, he was a man to whom the precise technical terms of other men's trades were important.

'10. Thursday. Three of our fleet being far ahead and to the leeward, supposed to be strangers, had chase given them by order from the Generals. The same day a small man of France that came from the coast of Spain came into the fleet and went aboard the Admiral Howard with some reports of those parts, but not of consequence.

'11. Friday in the morning, the Lord Admiral Howard went aboard the Lord General Essex, upon whose coming the Queen's Arms, a flag appointed to be a token to call together the Selected Council, was hung on the mizzen shrouds at sight whereof the Council aforesaid, repaired to that ship, at which consultation the Admiral, Vice-Admiral and Rear Admiral of Holland were present, where it was projected in what manner the squadrons with their admirals should make their approach to the Bay of Cadiz, what places fit to land the companies, and in what manner to attempt the town and such ships and galleys as should be found in the Road; but yet not so concluded, but left to such further consideration as should be thought necessary upon view of the place.

'After dinner a flag of St. George (a token assigned to call a Common Council of captains and masters) was hanged in the shrouds as before, upon whose repair these questions were propounded:

'First, what height we were in, which for the most part was taken to be next to 42 degrees to the southward.

'Secondly, how many leagues they supposed the fleet at that instant to be west from the shore. Their opinions were sundry, but the greatest part of the masters supposed about 30 leagues.

'Thirdly, what course were best to be sailed for the doubling of Cape St. Vincent, which, after long debating, our course was resolved to hold south and by east, whereof all the captains and masters were willed to take knowledge, with commandment to attend diligently upon the Admiral of their particular squadrons.'[7]

Reckoning latitude presented comparatively little difficulty in good weather. Jan van Doornik, the Admiral of Holland's kinsman, who kept a log-book on the Dutch flagship (see Appendix II), noted on 11/21 June:

> 'At 43 degrees, at the height of Cape Finisterre, the wind North by West, we were at a guess 28 leagues off land, in the afternoon shot 42⅓ degrees. At night got the wind at North North-East with clear weather.'[8]

He, like his English friends, was estimating how far to the east land lay, because the accurate measurement of longitude at sea, before the invention of the chronometer, was extremely difficult.

> 'To take a latitude
> Sun, or stars, are fitliest view'd
> At their brightest, but to conclude
> Of longitudes, what other way have we
> But to mark when, and where the dark eclipses be?'[9]

Donne had seen his commanding officer, the Earl of Essex, using a beautiful dial of brass with which he could take midnight readings from the constellation of the Little Bear, calculate tides and make many other predictions.[10] This bore a London maker's name, Kynvyn, and, with its various leaves closed, fitted comfortably into the palm of a man's hand, providing an astronomical calendar for the 35 years 1593–1627. Ordinary shipmasters found such dials too expensive, and preferred to buy printed tables and use them in conjunction with a simple pocket-size ring dial.

For the geography of the coast squadron commanders could refer to a translation of a book of charts entitled *Spieghel der Zeevaerdt* by Lucas Jenszoon Wagenaer, known to English seamen by the affectionate name 'waggoners'. Wagenaer, a native of Enkuizen, a port on the Zuider Zee, was self-taught. Without the benefit of university education, he had acquired the theoretical and practical knowledge needed by the pilots of his country, and had invented a means of training rough seamen in scientific methods of ascertaining their position at sea. His books were particularly popular because they had been printed in the clear Roman type invented by Christopher Plantin, who at one time prospered in Antwerp by printing prayer books ordered by Philip II. The English translation of the *Spieghel*, entitled *The Mariners Mirrour*, had been prepared by Antony Ashley and published in 1588 with a dedication to the Lord Chancellor of the day, Sir Christopher Hatton. This contained twenty-three charts showing the coasts of northern Europe, eastern and southern England, France, Portugal and Spain down to Cadiz, and included sailing directions, tide tables and almanacs. The entrances to rivers, ports and havens were not drawn to scale, but were diagrams with illustrations showing such landmarks as hills, beacons, trees and churches. Users were asked to record on their copies information found by sounding. (The sea bed often shifts in great storms and depths vary.) Sounding leads were hollowed out at the base, and the cavity filled with tallow, to which shells, gravel, sand or ooze clung, revealing in fog, darkness or foul weather those well-known differences in the sea bed that told a captain which side of the Channel he was on.

> 'Who ever yet could sound thy bottom? find
> The ooze, to show what coast thy sluggish crare
>     might easiliest harbour in? . . .'[11]

A Spanish gentleman, referring to this practice, remarked jestingly to Carew and Raleigh's friend, Sir Arthur Gorges, that the English 'raked hell for their sailing instructions', whereas his countrymen cast eyes aloft to the heavens, meaning that they navigated by the stars.

The Council next turned its attention to supplies:

> '[11] And further that the Regiments might not be unprovided of munitions, direction was given by the Lords Generals unto the Master of Ordnance to deliver unto every Colonel a convenient proportion. After all which the Council, captains and masters parted.

58

'This day also a commission was delivered under the Lords Generals' hands and directed to Sir George Carew, Master of the Ordnance, to Antony Ashley, secretary for the Council of War, and Marmaduke Dorrell, Victualler-General for the army, to this tenure ensuing.'[12]

The munitions which Sir George was here authorised to distribute had been loaded during April in four ships, *Experience*, *Phoenix*, *Brownfish* and *Humfry*.[13] According to the report compiled by Captain Slingsby *Experience* sailed with Raleigh, *Phoenix* with Essex, and *Brownfish* with Lord Thomas Howard. *Humfry* does not appear among those in the Admiral's squadron, but she may have been the vessel Slingsby calls the hoy of Sandwich. The gunpowder was in hundredweight (112 lb) casks, 24 of which went to a last; these had to be opened with a brass tool to avoid the danger of sparks. Enormous quantities of powder were consumed in a gun battle because the weight of the charge used for each firing was about half the weight of the 'pellet' or shot, and sometimes more. Almost all the guns were smooth-bore muzzle-loading pieces. Barrels, each being cast in a separate mould and in-dividually drilled, varied in weight. 'Twenty-eight hundredweights is the normal weight of a ship's demi-culverin', wrote Sir George Carew to Sir Robert Cecil in July 1594, 'but the founders never cast so exactly but their pieces vary 2 to 3 cwts.'[14] Demi-culverins fired a 9 lb shot and were the most popular weapons in the fleet. As Lieutenant of the Ordnance Sir George 'put to the proof' new gun barrels sent to London by the gunfounders of Buxted in Sussex, and elsewhere. This was done on Woolwich marshes or Black-heath, first with a small charge and then a larger; being fired with a full charge, about one in ten burst. Nevertheless, English guns were considered so good that they were bought by the Spaniards.

To load a gun from the muzzle was a complicated operation because the powder charge, whether wrapped in cartridge paper or not, had to be inserted separately and followed by a wad of rags to pack the charge into the breech. The shot was then rammed in, followed by a second wad. In action loading a gun heated by previous firing was dangerous, because the charge might be ignited prematurely by a smouldering rag left in the barrel. To prevent

59

this, barrels were swabbed out between firings. The word breech meant nothing more than the rear end of the gun barrel, where there was a narrow touchhole drilled just above the place where the charge lay. Before firing, this had to be filled with a small quantity of loose powder. When the order was given to fire, a gunner, standing to one side of the gun, lowered his lighted linstock[15] on to the powder in the mouth of the touchhole and the fire ran down into the charge. Without a linstock a gunner was in danger of being hit by the gun's recoil. The following instructions, taken from Cyprian Lucar's *Art of Shooting* printed in London in 1588, and dedicated to the Earl of Leicester, are a translation of a much earlier Italian work by Tartaglia, with some later material added. It applied equally to naval guns.

'A Gunner that hath a charge ought always to have in readiness all necessary things for his artillery: that is to say, wheels, axletrees, ladles, rammers, sponges, gunpowder, canvas or paper for cartridges and fireworks, forms for ladles and cartridges, needles and thread to sew and bind the cartridges and fireworks, artificial torches, candles, lanthorns, mattocks, shovels, crows and iron, handaxes, levers, engines for mounting and imbasing of ordinance, ropes, little handbaskets, glue or paste . . . and a sufficient number of Gunners and assistants to charge, discharge, mount, imbase, wad, ram, make clean, scour and cool his pieces when they are overheated, and to have for this purpose vinegar and fair cold water . . .

'[When no cartridges are available] put first your hand into the gunpowder which you have prepared to charge the piece, and perceiving thereby that the same powder is dry, fill the ladle belonging to the piece that shall be charged full of the same gunpowder so many times as is requisite, and evermore with your hand, or some other thing, strike away all the dry gunpowder that shall be above the brim or sides of the same ladle. Then, mounting the piece to six or seven degrees, and, standing upon one side of the piece (because it is a perilous thing to place your whole body right against the mouth of a piece which, charged with gunpowder, may through many occasions go off suddenly) put the said ladle so filled with dry gunpowder into the lowest end of the said concavity, and when you have so done, turn within the piece the upside of the ladle down, so as the gunpowder may fall into the piece . . .

'Also thrust a big wad of tow, hay, straw or of untwisted ropes into the piece home unto the charge in gunpowder for to sweep and keep together all the said charge in gunpowder, and to cause the pellet that shall be shot out of the same piece to range far.

'Also if you will in time of service charge any of the said pieces of Artillery with cartridges, do thus: Put first a cartridge into the mouth of the piece, and then with a rammer thrust it into the lowest end of the piece's concavity, and next drive a wooden tampion with a rammer into the same concavity home to the cartridge, then join a good big wad of hay, straw, tow, or of untwisted ropes, into the said tampion and put a fit pellet into the piece close unto the said wad; and when the piece so charged [is to] shoot downwards at a mark, thrust another like big wad into his concavity hard upon the pellet. This done, put a long pricker into the touchhole of the piece so charged and with the same pricker pierce divers holes through the cartridge lying within the piece or (which in mine opinion is a better device) cut clean away before you do put the cartridge into the hollow cylinder a piece of the outside of the cartridge in that part which shall lie directly under and next unto the touchhole.

'[Without a ladle or cartridge] throw the gunpowder into the piece with your hands until by estimation the piece hath received thereof a due charge, and with a rammer thrust the same gunpowder down into the bottom of the piece . . . Then measure with a stick ready marked.

'[To make gunmatches] take cords made of hemp that is not very fine, or of tow, which is better, although it will sooner consume, and let every cord be so big as a man's great finger. Also choose such cords for this purpose as are not much wreathed. This done, boil the same cords in strong lie, ashes, and a little saltpetre till all the lie shall be consumed . . . Touch the train of gunpowder by the touchhole of the piece with a linstock or a fired gunmatch (which some Gunners do tie to the end of a stick of three or four foot in length, and some Gunners do set fast in the cocks of their staves, and some Gunners do wind about the staff end of an halberd or partisan.'

'[To make cartridges] make upon a long and round mould, or form, of wood, a long and round bag of paper, fustian or canvas. Let the round wideness of this bag be a little less than the circumference of the concavity in the piece that shall shoot this cartridge and make the length of this bag equal to the just length of the ladle which belongeth to the piece that shall shoot the cartridge. Moreover fashion this bag with a round flat bottom, and then, putting into the same bag so much gunpowder as the piece which shall shoot this bag requireth for his due charge, shut up the upper end or mouth of the bag and, when you will afterwards put this bag of gunpowder (which among Gunners is called a cartridge) into the bore or concavity of any gun, remember to cut clean away (before you do put it into a gun) that piece of the bag which shall lie directly under and next to the touchhole of the gun, to this end, that only by putting fire unto the gunpowder in the touchhole you may without any fail give fire to all the gunpowder in the said bag or cartridge.

'When you will make a bag for a cartridge upon a mould or form and paste or glue together the sides of the same bag, anoint well with tallow that part of the said form which shall lie under the paste or glue, and suffer the bag to remain upon his form till the paste or glue shall be thorough dry, for, in drawing the said form out of the bag, you shall see that the bag will then cleave to no part of the anointed form.'

The black gunpowder then used was a mixture of one half saltpetre (potassium nitrate), one third charcoal and one sixth sulphur. Elizabethan gunners did not understand that its burning rate does not change with variation of pressure, and, hoping to make their weapons more effective, habitually overcharged them. They also believed, wrongly, that a long-barrelled gun would shoot further with the same weight of powder and shot than a short-barrelled one,[16] a belief shared, until recently, by modern writers, because a modern long-barrelled gun using a smokeless nitrocellulose propellant does shoot further than one with a short barrel. In the sixteenth century master gunners were the most highly paid members of the armed forces and tended to exaggerate the effectiveness of their weapons, stressing their maximum range, not their maximum effective range. John Sheriffe, for example, published artillery tables in 1590 giving the 'point blank' range of the long-barrelled demi-culverin as 400 paces and the 'extreme' range at 2,500. For the demi-cannon, firing a 30 lb 4 oz shot with an 18 lb charge he gave a point blank range of only 340 paces and an extreme range of 1,700 paces.[17] One Italian encyclopedia, printed in 1603, gave maximum ranges that could only have been obtained with muzzle velocities of 6,000 feet per second, about five times the speed of sound and almost three times the muzzle velocities of modern small arms.[18]

There were other reasons for bad shooting. Cannon-balls rusted quickly, especially at sea, and when the rust had been removed, fitted even more loosely into the barrel than new ones. The varying amount of windage was difficult to judge and gunpowder was too scarce a commodity for gunners to be given any for practice. Before he left Essex had received a profoundly depressing letter from Lord Willoughby, under whom he had served in France:

'Her Majesty may be served at better rates than she is considering what privileges they have for saltpetre making. The merchants buy it of our neighbour countries for 7d or 8d the lb, and it is issued here for 14d or 15d the lb, sometimes above; commonly for 10d and 12d the middle sort. Very honourable orders have been taken by the Lords [of the Council] for training the common soldiers; but practising men to use artillery is not hitherto seen into, so that mean and handicraft persons have for small sums crept into those rooms fit for ancient practised soldiers and perfect mathematicians. These, if set to make a breach or defeat the ranks and squares of a "battaile", can as soon hit the sun as the mark they shoot at.'[19]

Dr. Marbecke, being a non-combatant and a man of most lively intelligence, was enjoying the novelty of the sights and sounds around him with a truly boyish pleasure. On 2 May, soon after he arrived in Plymouth, he had seen the man in *Mary Rose* ducked at the main yard arm[20] and found out that he had been 'in the bilboes' for picking and stealing from his companions. After ducking he had been set ashore with a can of beer, a pound of bread and a pound of candles and told to fend for himself. Now, off the coast of Portugal, standing on the upper deck of *Ark Royal* with Sir William Leonard, the doctor saw flying fishes for the first time and 'took great delight to see the Dolphins and Bonitos coursing one of another in manner of a playing at Base which is a very pretty sight to behold, the said Bonitos and Dolphins seeming to be in size about the bigness of a young calf'.[21]

'[11] Also this day about 3 of the clock in the afternoon', Sir George noted, 'three flyboats, two of Amsterdam and one of Middelburg, were taken after some resistance made to the *True Love*, whereof Master Richard Levenson was captain, who did first hail them and by the aid of the *Lioness*, wherein Sir Christopher Blount was transported. These flyboats came directly from Cadiz loaded with salt, wines etc. and homeward bound, and in them was found in barrels silver [space left blank] and in bags, gold [space left blank] There was killed of the Flemings in the Admiral,[22] who made greatest resistance, 3 men, whereof the master was one, and sundry hurt, and gave some intelligence of the state of Cadiz, where there is no preparation extraordinary for their defence, for that, as they reported, they were persuaded that our land and sea forces were to be employed for defence at home, and that when they came from thence there was 13 sail of Spanish ships and one great Dane outward bound deeply laden for the Indies. 10 of the king's ships of war, the *St. Philippo* being Admiral, were in a readiness at St. Lucar to fall into the Bay of Cadiz to accompany these merchants for their guard to the Indies.'[23]

When this news filtered through the fleet Dr. Marbecke was amazed:

'What a sudden rejoicing there was through the whole army. Now every man skipt and leapt for joy, and how nimble every man was to prepare himself in the best manner and to see that all things were neat, trim and ready against the fight, fearing all the way that they should never have been encountered, or else have had sport as they used to term it.'[24]

The expedition's commanders did not share in this jubilation. *St. Philippo* had been with the convoy guard that surprised *Lion*, *Crane*, *Revenge*, and three others under Lord Thomas Howard's command at Flores in the Azores in 1591. Many of the English crews had been on shore when warning came. Lord Thomas gave the signal for retreat, but Sir Richard Grenville in *Revenge* disobeyed. According to Raleigh, 'out of the greatness of his mind, he could not be persuaded'. His ship surrounded, Sir Richard was severely wounded, and forty of the crew killed. The survivors, almost all wounded, refused an order to blow up their ship, surrendered, and carried their captain aboard the Spanish admiral's ship, where he died three days later. Whether he was buried at sea or on land is not known. This was the first time a Queen's ship had been lost to the Spaniards. The cause, disobedience, was forgotten and the memory of her last fight was kept green, first by Raleigh and, long afterwards, by Tennyson. It was Raleigh's object at Cadiz to 'revenge the *Revenge*'.[25]

The presence of the Anglo-Dutch fleet off the coast was not known to the enemy. If Cadiz were still to be taken by surprise a fair wind was essential, so that it was with satisfaction that Sir George noted:

'12. Saturday, the weather fair and the wind very handy, at noon we found ourselves in 40 degrees and 50 minutes.

'13. Sunday in the morning about six of the clock upon our larboard side the Brelings appeared, which was the first land we made from our departure from Plymouth.'[26]

In his log Jan van Doornik described this landfall more fully:

'Came opposite the Berlingas which are five rocks situated near the river of Lisbon, on one of which was a monastery that was destroyed by the English a long time ago. With the wind at North North-East we proceeded South-East.'[27]

'[13] Towards night a caravel was taken and brought into our fleet, being a fisherman of Peniche. Also the same [day] athwart the Rock the *John and Francis*, wherein Master Dorrell the Victualler was captain, took a flyboat called the *Falcon* of Flushing, laden with oils and wine; in her was also silver [space left blank] of gold [space left blank]. She was laden in Majorca with Spanish goods and bound, as we supposed, for Lisbon. The *Swan*, wherein Master Richard Weston was captain, the night before laid this ship aboard, in which fight the master of the flyboat was slain and eight men hurt, and in Master Weston's ship 1 slain and 11 hurt,[28] but in the end the *Swan* broke her beak head and bolt sprit and fell off, but ere the prize could recover Lisbon, whither they said they intended to go to bury their master and to repair their harms, she was after laid aboard and taken as aforesaid by Master Dorrell.

'14. Monday. The flyboat taken by Master Dorrell the day before came into the fleet.'[29]

Two days after this fight Jan van Doornik records:

'A man from Flushing taken by the English, who fought twice, and with two other Dutchmen, and took from the two ships more than 370,000 guilders; what she took from the third, from Middleburg, is not known yet.'[30]

Neither found it worthy of comment that Dutch ships had been carrying on such a lucrative trade with the enemy in time of war. To discuss the intelligence gained from the Dutchmen,

'[14] Aboard Lord General Essex, the Selected Council did voluntarily meet where consultation was had in what manner the town should be attempted and the ships secured.[31] Also this day there was two caravels taken and the land of Montfigo was discovered.'

For a fleet to sail within range of land batteries and to fight enemy ships in the confined waters of a harbour was considered an exceedingly hazardous operation. When Drake attacked Cadiz in 1587, he led his ships in immediately, without holding a preliminary council of war or agreeing a plan of action with his captains. William Borough, his second-in-command, who withdrew and made for home when his ship was hit at a mile range by a shot from the shore, afterwards complained about Drake's conduct:

'We have served as witnesses to the words you have delivered; or else you have used us well by entertaining us with your good cheer, and we have departed as wise as we came.'[32]

Drake court-martialled him, in his absence, for desertion in face of the enemy, but the sentence was overruled.

Lord Howard of Effingham, in planning his attack, was faced with a much more difficult task than Drake because troop landings had to be synchronised with the movements of men-of-war. Essex raged when forbidden to take his ship into action. Orders from the Queen, Howard explained, forbade him to place the Earl in unnecessary danger.[33]

The extraordinary geography of the port of Cadiz was familiar to many of the seamen in the allied fleet. From ancient times it had provided traders from the Mediterranean, Africa and northern Europe with a refuge safe in all weathers. After the discoveries of Christopher Columbus and Vasco da Gama the big ships that made ocean voyages to the Spanish and Portuguese colonies began to favour it for careening, watering and replenishing stores. The inner and outer parts of this haven are formed by two wide bays which would be completely unprotected from the Atlantic if it were not for a long narrow isthmus of sand and rock running parallel to the coastline but four miles out to sea. On this natural breakwater is the town of Cadiz, its white, flat-roofed houses huddled together to keep the sunlight out of the narrow streets, and appearing to float like Venice on the edge of a vast lagoon. The Elizabethans always spoke of the Island of Cales because there was only one land exit, a sandy track that ran along the isthmus for four miles and then, skirting the inner harbour, crossed to the mainland by a fortified wooden bridge. Under the bridge ran a narrow waterway connecting the harbour with the open sea about ten miles south of the town. The sea entrance to the outer harbour, or road, is broad, but obstructed at one point by sandy shale and low rocks, some of them just below the surface at high water, and known from their hog's back shape as *Los Puercos*. The rise and fall of the tide varies between four and nine feet, and currents complicate navigation. The passage into the inner haven narrows down to a mile and a half, but leads to a vast expanse of water where a whole navy could safely ride at anchor. Saltpans round the edge of the bay provide the town

67

with a valuable export, formerly bought by ports not only in Spain and Portugal, but far away in northern Europe for curing fish.

Tunny fishing was a major industry at three mainland ports within easy reach of Cadiz, Rota to the north, Puerto Santa Maria across the bay on the estuary of the Guadalete, and, near the mouth of a river that enters the inner harbour, Puerto Real. All these had medieval walls of the kind that protected them from raids by pirates, but were useless against an army with artillery.

'15. Tuesday morning we doubled the Cape St. Vincent, and that day the *Roebuck* brought in a caravel to whom she had overnight given chase, but the men, to save themselves, ran aground and abandoned the vessel. That day the Lords and Council dined aboard the Vice-Admiral the Lord Thomas Howard, where consideration was had and direction under the Lords Generals' hands given to the Admirals of Squadrons etc., Colonels of Regiments in what order and form the Army should be landed as followeth:

'Aboard Her Majesty's Ship the *Mere Honour* the 15th of June required, ordered and resolved by the Generals in Council for the landing at Cadiz.

'That the Admiral of every squadron have all his boats belonging to his squadron in a readiness to land those men that are now in the ships of his squadron.

'That if he have two regiments to be landed by his said boats, he shall of those regiments land equal numbers for the first, second or as many times as the boats come to fetch the men.

'That every Colonel, being one of those that shall have the point at the landing, shall land a third part of his regiment, which third part shall be of his best men, and those to come without any ensign with them because no ensign shall be engaged till the place of descent shall be secured.

'That the said regiments shall observe the same order in the attempting the town or forces except other direction be given by the Generals, viz that ensigns be kept where the greatest body and strength of the troops is till the other third part have tried the possibility of the attempt.

'That the boats that shall land the troops shall all be

marshalled in rank according to such a front as the place of descent will permit, which order of march in rowing or sailing they shall precisely keep, no boat thrusting out of a hinder rank into a former, nor shrinking out of the former into a hinder, of which order such land men as command the troops and such sea men as direct the boats shall give a strict account.

'That all the boats in the hinder ranks shall have their eye on the boat that leadeth them, and all the boats in the first rank shall observe the boat that is appointed to be their guide and director, which boat shall carry either a St. George's flag or a white pennant in the prow and shall keep in the head of the first rank at the going-off from the ships.

'That when the drum that beateth the first rank shall beat a march, they shall row forward such a pace as the first leadeth, who shall be appointed to row no faster than the slowest boat may conveniently keep company, and, if the leading boats stay and the drums cease beating, then shall they all stay, or, if the said leading boat lead backward, or turn her course some other way, he shall do the like.

'The first boats, being landed, shall be led to a fit place to make a stand to secure the ground of descent till the ensigns and the gross be landed.

'That, when the Admiral at the landing place shall receive his white pennant and set it above his flag on the main top, then shall the soldiers put themselves into boats to be landed as it shall be set down.'[34]

For landing operations, signals had to be pre-arranged between the ships and the boats. From a ship, lying, say, 600 yards out, only the backs of the breakers can be seen and so the surface of the sea appears to stretch in a level plain to the point where it meets the land, and this makes it impossible for those on the ships to judge the force of the breakers even when they are high enough to overwhelm a boat. On the other hand, those in the boats, when in the trough between waves, cannot observe the progress of the leading boats or of the fighting on shore. They need a signal of recall from the ships if the leading boats have been unable to establish a beachhead.

'16. Wednesday in the morning a caravel was discovered unto whom the Lord Thomas Howard and certain ships of his squadron gave chase, and, being taken, there was found none but 12 Englishmen in her, sailors appertaining to Mr. Bromely's ship of London, which was then in Barbary to take in her merchandise, during which time these mariners bought this caravel to get purchase on the coast of Algarve. By them we understood that we were not discovered from the main[land].'[35]

Mr. Bromely's trade with the infidel, though intensely annoying to the Spaniards, was legitimate. Almost certainly his ship was awaiting a cargo of saltpetre. The Shereef, as the English called the ruler of Morocco, possessed mines which produced the major constituent of gunpowder and exacted a high price for it in guns, small arms and cannon balls. The twelve English seamen were part-time pirates, wealthy enough to buy a ship with which to raid the Algarve. This caused no surprise because many of the crews in the Anglo-Dutch fleet had been on similar 'voyages of purchase' themselves.

'17. Thursday. As since the thirteenth of this month, the wind held fair at east and calmy, insomuchas in all these days we could not get to the eastward of Cape St. Marie.

'18. Friday. In the morning very early from out of the *Ark* a strange ship was discovered to be in our fleet, who in the night unadvisedly fell into the same, and did her best to acquit herself out of it, but, after two shots made unto her from the Admiral, she came aboard him. She was a ship of Waterford that the day before came from Cadiz. She did assure us that we were not discovered on the coast, and that in Cadiz they lived in great security, not having any knowledge of our being at sea. By her also we understood that there was sixty in the road before Cadiz outward bound for the West Indies about 20 sails of merchants and six galleons of the king's, whereof the *St. Philippo* was Admiral to waft them in their voyage; and further, either 14 or 16 galleys in St. Mary Port and Cadiz whereof divers of them were not yet in a readiness for the sea. Also she gave us knowledge of two argosies bound for Lisbon that put to sea immediately after her. The same morning the Lord Generals in

Council met aboard the *Ark*, where order was given that the *Warspite*, the *Mary Rose*, the *Quittance*, the *Lioness*, the *True Love*, and divers others to the number of 17 sail, should tack about to the coast to meet with the argosies aforesaid. And also in Council it was resolved that the Lord General Essex should land as it should please him to direct the land forces for the attempting of the town of Cadiz, and the Lord Admiral Howard with the best of the ships of war should at his direction give upon the ships there in the Road, or to guard them from escape until the town were surprised, and likewise Captain Alexander Clifford with the *Rainbow*, the *Vanguard*, the *Alcedo*, the *Affection* and three hoys should come to anchor before St. Mary Port to assure the galleys there from doing annoyance to our fleet. Further this day towards evening the Lord Admiral Howard with certain ships gave chase to [half page left blank].

'19. Saturday. The fleet which was appointed to attend Sir Walter Raleigh, holding their course inward to the shore, about 9 a clock in the morning discovered to the eastward between 9 and 14 sail, whereof one of them was a great galleon who bore with our forefoot until she came within a league of us and then plied up for the weather.[36] Immediately after a mighty fog about 4 a clock fell so thick as it was not possible for one ship to descry another a cable length off. In this fog Sir George Carew and Captain Gifford, who had been aboard the Rear Admiral in his ship's boat, with much ado came aboard a small pinnace and by a clock at night by great hap lighted on the *Quittance*, Captain Gifford's ship, where, looking out for their Admiral's light, they espied one to windward which they followed, and before break of day ran so far that course as they were at 5 fathom water close aboard the shore to the east of Clixiona. In this course one of the Spanish fleet next sail to the *Quittance* came aground, supposed by the *Quittance* to be Sir Walter Raleigh's hoy, wherefore direction was given to a caravel formerly taken by our fleet to repair to the ship aground and to bring away her men and to burn her, but she, finding the same to be a Spaniard, bare room. The Admiral and five others whose light the *Quittance* had followed all night, by the break of day came within musket shot of her, and made to the ship aground, not daring to approach her for fear of the gross fleet which were a league to the weather of her. When they came to the wreck, they gave her no aid, but bore on their course to the west.'[37]

The thick fogs which descend on coastal areas in hot weather do not roll slowly across the surface and give warning of their approach, but in a few minutes fall like a blanket from the sky.

'20. Sunday morning. About 6 a clock we came to anchor with the whole fleet before Cadiz over against the Callette, or mid-draught and by the Castle of St. Sebastian, where we proposed to make our descent, but the Lords Generals, having consideration of the danger we should enter into in landing our companies by reason of the greatness of the billow, altered their purposes, and in this storm the *Rainbow*'s boat with 15 men was overturned.'[38]

Even the big ships suffered from the violence of the storm. Sir Francis Vere recalled: 'The wind was so great and the billows so high that the capstan being too strong for my men cast them against the ship's side and spoiled many of them.'[39]

'Towards the evening the Lord General Essex weighed his anchor, and fell into the bay, after whom the whole fleet followed, where at that present directly before the town, nothing was done more than the delivery of certain shot from the Spanish fleet and the town upon the *Repulse*, the *Mary Rose* and the *Alcedo*, which ships rode nearest unto them and answered them with the like salutations.'[40]

The landing parties had chosen high tide, which was at 7 a.m.[41] and it was decided to take no further action until high tide the next day.

### Chapter III Notes

1. The sea league, Portuguese in origin, was 4 Roman miles, 3.2 nautical or 3.7 statute miles, i.e. 5.9 km. The Spaniards reckoned 16⅔ leagues to a degree, but the Portuguese, followed by the Dutch, reckoned more accurately 17½. The English reckoned 20 leagues or 60 miles to the degree, neglecting the difference between Roman and English miles. The mean length of a degree of latitude is roughly 69 statute miles or 111 km. When, early in

the sixteenth century, the Portuguese and the Spaniards partitioned the globe between them, they did not know it was a spheroid, not a sphere, and the difference in their standards of measurement became a serious matter.

2. Room—the navigable water to the leeward of a sailing ship. Captain John Smith's *A Sea Grammar*, London, 1627, explains: 'When a ship sails with a large wind towards the land, or a fair wind into a harbour, we say she bears in with the land or harbour, and when she would not come near the land, but goes more Room-way (roomy) than her course, we say, she bears off.' (Hence the phrase for a ship waiting at a point of rendezvous, which is said 'to bear off and on', using the room to her lee to keep her position.)

3. Lambeth Codex 250.

4. Lambeth Codex 250.

5. John Donne, *The Storm*.

6. Lambeth Codex 250.

7. Lambeth Codex 250.

8. Kaiserl. Bibliothek Wien, Cod. MS 13,033 Suppl. 383 f.34a–39a.

9. John Donne, *A Valediction of a Book*.

10. British Museum S.1.2.47.

11. Shakespeare, *Cymbeline* IV ii 206–8.

12. Lambeth Codex 250.

13. Hatfield 199.42.

14. State Papers Domestic 1594.

15. Linstock, a staff about 3 ft long having a pointed foot to stick in the deck or the ground and a forked head to hold a piece of match cord.

16. In *The Spanish Armada*, Batsford, 1960, Prof. Michael Lewis remarks: 'The longest gun (and therefore longest-ranged gun) that the English could manage on shipboard was the 14-foot whole culverin with a bore of only 5½ inches and a round shot of only about 17 pounds.'

17. State Papers Domestic 1590.

18. Francis Guilmartin Jr., Assistant Professor of History, US Air Force Academy, *Gunpowder and Galleys*, Cambridge University Press, 1974.

19. Hatfield 176.29. There being no saltpetre mines in the British Isles, agents of the Tudor monarchs bought gunpowder secretly from mills in the Spanish Netherlands and smuggled it into England. Sir Thomas Gresham was one of the most successful of these agents. Philip II put a stop to this trade, so, to augment supplies, the Queen bought from a German, Captain Gerard Honrick, for the very high price of £300, a recipe for manufacturing saltpetre. Under the Captain's instruction 'saltpetre men' learnt to mix earth with animal excrement collected from

73

barns, stables, and dovecotes, add lime and ashes, expose it on a cool dry pavement and moisten it with urine. After the heaps had been turned over for a considerable period, saltpetre crystallised out. As soon as this manufactured saltpetre was available, English powder mills were set up, and Sir George Carew advised that their sites should be secure and not near ports that the enemy might raid.

The smell of saltpetre manufacture was appalling, and in October 1595 Sir George was asked to give the saltpetre men in the City of London Steelyard a 'safe' workshop.

20. 'The Marshall is to punish offenders and to see justice executed according to directions, as ducking at the yard's arm [suspended by a rope reeved through a block on the end of a yardarm and repeatedly ducked in the water], hauling under the keel, bound to the capstan or mainmast with a basket of shot about his neck, setting in the bilboes [long iron bars with sliding shackles that hold the ankles] and to pay the Cobtie [be beaten with a barrelstave] or the Morion [military punishment, beating with a pikestaff]. But the boys the Boatswain is to see every Monday at the chest to say their compass [to box the compass, to recite the 32 major compass points] and receive their punishment for all their week's offences: which done, they are to have a quarter can of beer and a basket of bread. But if the Boatswain eat or drink before he catch them, they are free.' (Captain John Smith, *A Sea Grammar*, London, 1627.)

21. Rawlinson D124. 'The Quartermasters for fishing have a seine, a fingig [fishing spear] haarpin iron [harpoon] and fish hooks for Porges, Bonetos or Dorados and rayling lines for Mackerele.' (Captain John Smith, *A Sea Grammar*, London, 1627.)

22. Admiral—derived from Arabic *amir al*, commander of the, and hence applied to the commander's ship, however small the fleet.

23. Lambeth Codex 250.

24. Rawlinson D124.

25. Raleigh, *A Relation of Cadiz*, published by his grandson in 1699.

26. Lambeth Codex 250.

27. Kaiserl. Bibliothek Wien, Cod. MS. 13,033 Suppl. 383 f.34a–39a.

28. 'In an extremity a man would rather blow up the quarter deck, half deck, forecastle or anything than be taken by him he knows a mortal enemy, and commonly there is more men lost in entering (if the chase stand to her defence) in an instant than in a long fight board and board . . . I confess the charging upon trenches and the entrance of a breach in a rampire are attempts as desperate as a man would think could be performed; but he that hath tried himself as oft in the entering a resisting ship as I have done, both them and the other, he would surely confess there is no such dangerous service ashore as a resolved, resolute fight at

sea.' (Captain John Smith, *A Sea Grammar*, London, 1627.)
29. Lambeth Codex 250.
30. Kaiserl. Bibliothek Wien, Cod. MS. 13,033 Suppl. 383 f.34a–39a.
31. The details of the first plan of attack, entered in the Journal, but later crossed through, were:
    'Raleigh with all his squadron should enter into the Bay of Cadiz as far as Puntal, as well to surprise the merchant ships outward bound for the Indies as to land the regiments of the Earl of Essex and Sir Richard Wingfield at that isthmus not far from Puntal, where the land is narrowest. It was likewise agreed that Lord Thomas Howard on the south side of the aforesaid isthmus should land the two regiments of Sir Christopher Blount and Sir Thomas Gerrard, which 4 regiments are to be commanded by such persons, and to follow as the Lord Generals shall then appoint, the cause of whose employment on that part is to forbid any forces from the land to rescue the town of Cadiz at that side. The Lords Generals themselves not yet resolved what course to take in their own persons, but according as occasion should be ministered. Between St. Sebastian and the block house of Los Puercos, in the bay of Catalina, it was resolved the Lord General Essex'
32. State Papers Domestic 1587.
33. Hatfield 47.99.
34. Lambeth Codex 250.
35. Lambeth Codex 250.
36. 'If he be right ahead of you that is called a stern chase, if you weather him [get to his windward], for every man in chasing doth seek to get the weather because you cannot board him except you weather him . . .' (Captain John Smith, *A Sea Grammar*, London, 1627.)
37. Lambeth Codex 250.
38. Lambeth Codex 250.
39. *An English Garner*, Vol. VII, 1883.
40. Lambeth Codex 250.
41. Commander N. C. Glen, R.N., Superintendent of Tidal Branch in the Department of the Hydrographer of the Navy, kindly supplied the authors with the following 'predictions':
    Cadiz 20th June (Old Style)
    Low Water 0040 hours   High Water 0700
    Low Water 1300 hours   High Water 1930
The correction to convert these to Local Mean Time, which is probably nearer the time kept in the ship's journal, is minus 25 minutes.
    The 20th June 1596 was two days after spring tides. The mean spring range at Cadiz is 2.7 metres; the mean neap range 1.3 metres.

# IV

# Assured of the Victory

In Cadiz nobody slept. Some householders carried heavy stones to their upper rooms and rooftops ready to hurl down on the heads of troops invading the streets below.[1] With the meagre forces on hand, they had little hope that the town walls could be held, since, instead of rebuilding them in the new style required to resist artillery, banks of earth had been thrown up to protect the old masonry from bombardment. The 'castle' or citadel built in one corner of the walls was equally indefensible. Relief from the mainland was out of the question. Not all the gold and silver in Seville could provide it, for the great city was ninety miles away at the head of the long estuary of the Guadalquivir, and any reinforcements from there would have to fight their way in. Nor was the safety of the people of Cadiz the only concern of the Spanish authorities. The Indies fleet with its cargoes represented an enormous investment by the *Casa de Contratacion* in Seville, a Government commission which controlled the whole of Spain's overseas trade. Its president, Senor Pedro Guttieres Flores, was in Cadiz on the morning of Sunday, 20 June, and woke to see the Anglo-Dutch armada at anchor in the roadstead north of the town. *'Una hermosissima vista'* (a most beautiful sight), he wrote with reluctant admiration. There was no way of escaping disaster. Another Spanish eyewitness described the citizens as smitten with the numbness of despair, appearing *'Muertos antes de morir, cadaveres antes de espirar'* (dead before dying, corpses before expiring).[2] At sunrise observers in the town saw skiffs going alongside *Ark Royal*, but no signs of any further attempt to land troops.

'21. Monday. In the morning after sun rising the Lords Generals and Council met aboard the *Ark*, where it was resolved that the

Lord Thomas Howard, Vice-Admiral of the fleet, in the *Nonpareil*, Sir Walter Raleigh, Rear Admiral, in *Warspite*, the Lord Marshal in the *Rainbow*, the Master of the Ordnance in the *Mary Rose*, Sir John Wingfield in the *Vanguard*, Sir Robert Southwell in the *Lion*, Alexander Clifford in the *Dreadnought* and Captain Cross in the *Swiftsure*, with certain merchants and Dutch men-of-war should fight with the fleet, the Lords Generals with the rest of the fleet to be under sail, but not to come in danger or to fight unless the ships recited were distressed. While this was in Council determining, the Spanish fleet weighed and came under sail, falling further into the bay towards Port Real, the merchant ships running up the river as far as they could, and the king's ships with others stayed at anchor over against Puntal, guarded with all the galleys except two left close by Cadiz.'[3]

The station chosen by the Spanish Admiral was in the passage between the inner and outer harbour where there was not enough deep water for more than a third of the allies' men-of-war to operate. Even so, the odds against him were overwhelming.

'[21] Sir Walter Raleigh, having weighed sooner than the rest, made after them, leading our fleet in with great bravery, and in passing by the town, infinite store of shot was spent between our ships, the town and galleys, much to their damage and nothing to our loss. When we were come within a reasonable distance of the enemy where they were at anchor, we likewise anchored, and rode as conveniently as the straitness of the channel would permit, and immediately a furious battery on either side was entertained. The ships of ours on whom the substance of the fight did consist were ten sail. The next to the Admiral of Spain was Sir Walter Raleigh. To second him not long after the battery began, my Lord General Essex, contrary to the former resolution, continued in his course and came in his own ship to anchor close by Sir Walter Raleigh, changing shot for shot abundantly, then the Lord Marshal, then Sir George Carew; after him my Lord Thomas Howard in the *Nonpareil*, then Sir Robert Southwell, Captain Clifford, Captain Cross and the *Alcedo*. And after the fight had continued a good while, my Lord

77

Admiral, understanding that the Earl of Essex was gone in, being unable to come in with his own ship pestered up with the gross of the fleet afar off, went aboard the *Mere Honour*, who by that time was in fight.[4]

'About six a clock in the morning the fight in our passage by the town and galleys did begin. About 9 the galleys rowed to the great ships to give them aid, but, within one hour after, the galleys shrank for their guard and fell under Puntal, which fort did beat us afar off with their ordnance.

'About one a clock in the afternoon the enemy weighed to withdraw themselves further into the river. Whereupon the Generals resolved to board them, but so many in their ships were slain and every man so much dismayed, as neither did soldier attend to his piece nor mariner to his service, whereby their ships ran aground, and, before we could come to them, their men, leaping into the water, were drowned in great numbers, and those that escaped ran to Port Real.

'The substance of the enemy's fleet was 4 of the king's armadoes, to say: the *St. Philippo* Admiral [Captain Diego de Sotomayor]; the *St. Matteo* Vice-Admiral [Don Juan de Alcega]; the *St. Andrea* and the *St. Tomaso*; two great galleons which came from Lisbon: 3 great frigates of the king's; the Admiral, Vice-Admiral and Rear Admiral of New Spain, which last Admiral [*La Capitana*: Don Diego Alfonso Flores, Captain General of the Indies fleet] was the greatest ship in all the fleet; three Ragusans,[5] in all, ships of war 21, and of merchants about 40 sail more, besides 19 galleys of the best in Spain namely the

| | |
|---|---|
| *Capitana*: | the Admiral in whom was Don Juan de Puertocarrero, lieutenant to the Adelantado and brother to the Conde de Palma |
| *Occasion*: | in whom was Captain the Marques de St. Croce: Captain Christophero de Sanches |
| *Padiglia*: | Captain Juan de Osorio, Conde de Bracamonte |
| *Patrona*: | Captain Don Diego de Mendoza, nephew to the duke of Infantasgo |
| *Fama*: | Captain Julian Hortado |
| *Eugenia*: | Don Gonsalvo |
| *Luna*: | Captain Medina |

| | |
|---|---|
| *Manrique*: | Don Garsia |
| *St. Barbara*: | Captain Alcate |
| *Lucera*: | Captain Colero |
| *Espagnola*: | |
| *Leona*: | Ernando de Sarita |
| *Bassan*: | Don Antonio de Jubilatar |
| *Fortezza*: | |
| *Esperanza*: | Diego Ordonez |
| *Temeraria*: | Captain Sepeda |
| *Lieva*: | Pedro Vargas |
| *Serena*: | Captain Badillo |
| *St. Yago*: | Juan de Arango |

19

The loss that we received in this sea service was one flyboat unfortunately fired by negligence by some of the same ship and not 30 slain by the enemy and of them but one gentleman, son to Customer Smyth: besides one other pinnace of Sir Robert Southwell, which, in laying the great ship aboard whilst she was burning, was fired by her, the men all saved[6] and all their ships were laden richly and bound for the Indies. Among those that came aground the *St. Philippo* and the *St. Tomaso* set themselves presently on fire, to our exceeding glory and joy, thereby assured of the victory. The *St. Matteo* and *St. Andrea* were left on ground, abandoned by them and taken by us.'[7]

The Admiral, Don Diego de Sotomayor, had followed the grim custom of the service in setting fire to his ship rather than let her fall into enemy hands, and his example was followed by his Vice-Admiral in *St. Tomaso*. John Donne saw the ghastly consequences:

'Out of a fired ship, which, by no way
But drowning, could be rescued from the flame,
Some men leap'd forth, and ever as they came
Near the foes' ships, did by their shot decay;
So all were lost, which in the ship were found,
They in the sea being burnt, they in the burnt ship drown'd.'[8]

'[21] This done, the Lord General Essex did instantly ship into long boats and pinnaces about 3,000 of his land companies of every regiment a part, accompanied with most of the officers and gentlemen that were for land service, landing them in a little bay between Puntal and Cadiz, and from thence marched directly to the south side of the island. The enemy from the town, beholding our troops, sallied forth both horse and foot to impede our approach unto it, the Lord General, thinking by their countenance they purposed to fight, advanced part of his force towards them, for Sir Conyers Clifford, Sir Christopher Blount and Sir Thomas Gerrard with their regiments were sent to secure the strait of the land which was not far from us. Sir John Wingfield, leading in the vanguard, was charged by the enemy's horse, who stood them bravely, and with his pike wounded Don Nunno de Villa Vincenza, one of the chiefest cavaliers. The enemy, finding our stand so firm, retreated in rout to the port of the town, pressing to get in to the same in such haste as they left many of their horses behind them.

'The Lord General Essex evermore with the foremost, having now won the ditch, in gaining whereof some men were lost, and Sir John Wingfield and Captain Merkyrk shot, ascended the rampart and caused his own colours to be first advanced upon the wall. At sight whereof the enemy fled and divers of our men, some over the wall, [and] some at the corner of the wall, entered, who opened the port for the General. In every street resistance was made with loss on either side, even unto the market place, where in like manner from the tops of the houses and windows they shot many of our men and amongst the rest (long after we were possessed of that place) Sir John Wingfield was slain. The Lord Marshal in the meantime, with some soldiers, led towards the Priory, whereunto divers men of good quality were fled for succour, who upon honour rendered themselves that night.'[9]

Sir Francis Vere, who warmly commended Essex's leadership, afterwards said:

'The ditch was very hollow, but dry, out of which was raised a massy rampire . . . in height and thickness in their perfection, but not steeped or scarped, so it was very mountable, and lay

7. Astronomical Ring made by Succa for the Cardinal Archduke Albrecht. (*Oxford Museum of the History of Science*)

8. Pocket Dial of the Earl of Essex made in London 1593 by Kynvyn. A navigational instrument with astronomical calendar for the years 1593 to 1627. (*Reproduced by courtesy of the Trustees of the British Museum*)

9. The Channel coast between Portland and Plymouth, from
Sir Antony Ashley's *The Mariner's Mirrour*, 1588.
(Published by permission of the British Library)

When you fayle there alongst two leagues of.

The Shewing of S. Aldams land or Coast. When it is two leagues from you.

PARS.

Waymouth

Porth

Mount

East Chald

PTENTRIO. N.

ORIENS. E.

North or by East.
North North East.
North East & by North
North East.
North East & by East.
East North East.
East & by North.
East & by South.
East South East
South East by East
South East
South East & by South
South East by East

OF

ND

Burport

Sandesfoote Castle

The Raff

Portland

The Ras of Portland

A, DESCRIPTION OF THE
Sea coastes of England.
Betweene Plymouth &
Portland. With the
cheefest hauens thereof,
according vnto theire
Situation

11. Jan van Duivenvoorde, Admiral of Holland, Lord of Warmond, by Golzius, commemorating his relief of Leiden in 1579 during the War of Independence against Spain. (*Rijksmuseum, Amsterdam*)

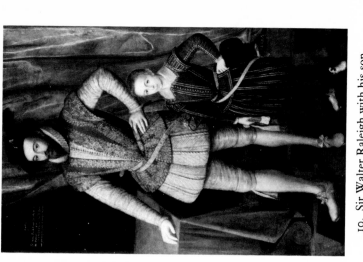

10. Sir Walter Raleigh with his son about 1602. (*National Portrait Gallery, London*)

close to the old wall of the town, which somewhat overtopped it no higher than in many places a man might reach with his hand. To the top of the rampire our men climbed, who, being for the most part old and experienced soldiers of the Bands I brought out of the Low Countries, boldly attempted to climb the wall from which they beat with their shot the defendants. . .

'Wanting no encouragement that good example of the chiefs could give them, the General himself being as forward as any, I sent a Captain and countryman of mine called Upsher with some few men alongst the ditch to see what guard was held along the wall towards the Bay-ward; and whether any easier entrance might be made that way or not . . .

'My Lord of Essex was one of the first that got over the walls, followed by the soldiers as the place would give them leave; and such was their fury, being once entered, that, as they got in scatteringly, so they hasted towards the town without following into any strong and orderly body of men as in such case is requisite, or once endeavouring to open the gate. I therefore held the third body of the men together and with much ado brake open the gate by which I entered the town.

'Though I was slackly and slenderly followed by reason of our men's greediness for spoil, yet such Spaniards as I found making head I drove back into the Fort St. Philip and the Abbey of St. Francis. Those in the Abbey yielded to the number of 200 gentlemen and others . . . The brunt of this exploit was borne with less than 1,000 men . . . it seemed rather an inward tumult and town fray than a fight of so mighty nations.'[10]

Few young generals, holding command in battle for the first time, can have disobeyed orders so openly as Essex did at Cadiz. He took his ship into action in defiance of the Lord Admiral, and although, under the Selected Council's instructions, ensigns were forbidden to land until 'a head' had been made, he advanced his colours to the top of the rampart where a determined enemy might easily have captured them. On the other hand he had been in the right place at the right time, which is the essence of good generalship. Quick to see that about forty Spaniards, finding the town gate closed against them, had abandoned their mounts and run up the rampart, he ordered his men to do likewise and, seeing Sir John Wingfield was wounded in the thigh, ran forward to take his place. Sir John, having bound up his wound, seized a Spanish horse and joined in the fighting for the town square.[11]

'A strong guard was held for as yet the old town upper end wherein the castle is seated, and whereunto in a manner all the people of the town had put themselves.'

'The names of certain of the best sort that were in Cadiz when our fleet came before it:

Maximiliano de Austria, bishop elect of Cadiz, before Abbot of Alcala la Real in the kingdom of Granada: went to Seville

Don Antonio Sapeta, old bishop of Cadiz, elect bishop of Pamplona in Navarre: in Seville

Don Antonio de Raya, bishop of Cuzco in the kingdom of Peru: delivered freely[12]

Ernando de Guemes, a Biscayan, captain of the castle of Cadiz: delivered

Martin de Rigoien, a Biscayan, captain of the fort St. Philippo: delivered

Don Roderigo de Villa Vincenza, dean of Cadiz, employed to Seville with his brother [Don Bartholomeo] to procure the ransom of the rest, but never returned.

The prisoners' names:

Don Antonio Giron de Cuniga of the kingdom of Toledo Corregidor of Cadiz

Don Paio Patino, archdeacon of Cadiz

Pedro Guttieres Flores de Conseino de las Indias, president de la casa de la Contrastation de Indias de Criula

Pedro de Castylla Juas de las Indias in Cadiz

'Towards sun setting the Lord Admiral, the Lord Thomas Howard, Sir Walter Raleigh, and others whom we left aboard, came to us. The castle at Puntal immediately after our landing was by the guard abandoned and entered not by the Hollanders.[13] Captain Samuel Bagnell in this service deserved much honour, for he came often to the push of pike and was wounded in sundry places, in reward whereof that night the Lord General made him knight.[14] In winning of this town about

82

200 men—Sir Edward Wingfield, Sir Charles Percy, Captain Harvey, Captain Hambridge and others were hurt.'[15]

Captain Savage anticipated that the soldiers might avenge these casualties:

'I was sent, late in the afternoon by the Lords Generals into the castle with my Lord Essex' company of foot, of which I was lieutenant, to see no violence or wrong offered by the soldiers or other to any of the gentlewomen or the rest.'[16]

He and the company were forbidden to enter any house. The Spaniards were astonished at Essex's clemency and at the strictness with which he controlled his men, two being executed for attempted rape.[17] By an evil custom inherited from the middle ages it was common practice to massacre a population that refused to surrender on the first appearance of an enemy. The slightest show of resistance was held to justify this barbarous practice, and when Philip II heard how the women and religious of Cadiz had been spared and allowed to leave, he is reported to have said of Essex *'Tan hidalguia no si a vista entre herejes'* (Such chivalry is indeed not seen among the heretics).[18]

'22. Tuesday morning. Those at the town that had taken the castle for their safety hung forth a flag of truce and requested a treaty, which granted, the Corregidor and five others of the best amongst them came to the Generals and concluded with them, first, to yield to their mercy, offering for further composition to pay in regard of their lives 120,000 ducats and to put into their hands fifty of the best amongst them for pledges till the ransom should be paid, which being accepted, the Generals of their favour provided shipping to embark the women and religious persons to pass to Port St. Mary, and the meaner sort had convoy by land towards the bridge. This contract was interchangeably subscribed, and, to assure the return of these messengers to the castle from the violence of the soldiers, the Master of the Ordnance was commanded to convey there and to see the keys of the castle delivered to Captain Savage, to whom at that instant my Lord gave the honour of knighthood.

'The rest of this day till late night was spent in putting forth of

83

the castle the meaner sort and warning the rest. That done, the Captain of the fort of St. Philippo rendered the same and himself to the General's mercy.

'Also this day Sir Conyers Clifford, Sir Christopher Blount and Sir Thomas Gerrard with their regiments came into the town, who the day before had been sent to secure that strait of the land against such enemies as should be sent from the main[land] to assail us in the rearguard of our march to the town, who, as it should seem, mistaking his direction, marched on 12 miles to the bridge called Puente de Suaco, and in this journey they were greatly annoyed by a castle held by the Spaniards near to the bridge, by a barricado upon the fore end of the bridge and by the galleys drawn down to that place with purpose to pass through. All this not withstanding, they lodged there that night, destroyed some part of the bridge, and threw into the river two pieces of artillery that they found there. In the morning they retreated whom the enemy followed afar off, cutting the throats of such [of] our disordered soldiers as by drunkenness had disabled themselves either to march or move, so, as it is thought, we lost about 200 men, most thereof rather by their own default and drunkenness than by the enemy's sword. After the departure of our troops the king's galleys passed through the bridge and got a seaboard the Island and rowed to Rota.

'23. Wednesday. The gross of the Spanish fleet that escaped from us by running up towards Port Real, by the commandment of the Duke of Medina[19] were set on fire insomuchas of ships of war and merchants there was taken and burnt by us and them about 57 sail, the richest fleet that ever was bound for the Indies, being valued by estimation 12 million [ducats].'[20]

As an act of war, self-inflicted damage on such a scale was then rare, and its effects soon reached the heart of Old Castile. In the first half of Philip II's reign the merchants of Burgos, 150 miles north of Madrid, had built up a worldwide system of marine insurance, covering Spanish and Portuguese ships of all types and goods in transit to and from Asia, Africa and the Americas. The shipping losses of 1588 had been bad enough; now they had to bear at least part of the Cadiz compensation claims, and so both north and south were shattered simultaneously. One of Essex's spies, Guicciardini, wrote in the following spring that the King's credit was so diminished by the defeat at Cadiz that 'neither in Naples, Genoa or Milan can he find any that will disburse a penny, nor yet in Italy that will give accomplishment to the Cardinal's bills of exchange'.[21]

'24. Thursday. All the prisoners, the pledges excepted and such as were not comprised in the contract, were delivered under safe convoy. In the afternoon a Council was held at the Lord Generals' lodging, where it was disputed whether it was fit to keep this city or not, and concluded, by general opinion upon good reasons there alleged, that it was fit to be held, and to that purpose to dispatch a messenger to her Majesty, and in like manner Sir Edward Hoby to be sent forthwith into Barbary to the king of Morocco, as the Generals formerly had determined.'[22]

To Philip II such dealings with non-Christians were an abomination. His navy, victorious over the Turks at Lepanto in 1571, had saved the western Mediterranean from conquest by the Moslems. Now co-operation between the English and the rulers of North Africa seemed to him likely to expose the whole coastline of the Iberian peninsula to raiders of all kinds.

'[24] In this time of consultation, three captains of the galleys [came] with letters from Don Juan de Puertocarrero, Lieu-tenant-General for the Adelantado of Castile, to the Lords Generals, the contents whereof were to entreat the delivery of prisoners, either for ransom or exchange, in answer whereof the Lords dispatched Captain Robert Cross, Captain Watson and Captain Mydleton with their letters, signifying that already they had ransomed so many as they purposed: the ladies, and meaner people of either sexes, which were thousands in number, they had freely released. If he would send them the English prisoners in the galleys and elsewhere, they would take it in good part.

'25. Friday. Captain Cross with the rest returned [with] the answer that the Spaniards did promise to dispatch answer after him.

'26. Saturday. About 3 a clock in the afternoon there came a galley from the enemy called the *Lion* with his flag of truce, in whom Don Diego de Mendoza, a cavalier of Malta, and brother's son to the Duke of Infantasgo, the Conde de Ribadeo, Don Antonio de Veltrasio, son to the now Viceroy of Peru, Captain Pedro de Vergas and other gentlemen with letters from Don Juan de Puertocarrero to treat with the Generals for exchange of prisoners for such English captains as were in the galleys and elsewhere, which was agreed on either party.'[23]

The customs of war permitted the use of prisoners as forced labour, either in the galleys or elsewhere. If their captors judged that their families were unlikely to offer an acceptable ransom, knowledge of their fate might never reach home; their chances of 'returning from the dead' were slight. Suddenly the English prisoners in Cadiz had a value; they could be exchanged for Spanish noblemen. Some had been in captivity many years, others for a comparatively short time.

The Moroccans in the Spanish galleys had not waited for an exchange. At the height of the battle in the harbour, the English were astonished to see a number of oarsmen jump overboard and swim towards them. Their rescuers, happy to help men from a country regarded as an ally, provided a ship to carry thirty-eight of them home.[24]

'[26] After the departure of these Spanish gentlemen Sir John Wingfield was solemnly buried in the Cathedral Church of Cadiz. In his office of Camp Master Sir Christopher Blount succeeded; in his regiment Sir Horatio Vere; and in his ship, the *Vanguard*, Sir Robert Mansell.'[25]

Sir John had courted death in order to redeem a reputation that he imagined had been damaged in the Netherlands. When he was Governor of Gertruydenburg, the garrison, who had not received any pay for a long time, mutinied, locked Sir John up and accepted a large sum of money from the Spaniards for the surrender of the town. The Dutch held Sir John, not the troops, responsible and published slanderous pamphlets to that effect. He may have been a Catholic, since his successor as Camp Master, Sir Christopher

86

Blount, who was a Catholic, buried him with full military honours in the Cathedral.[26] For Donne, meditating on the scene, the great rocks on either side of the Straits of Gibraltar, known to the ancients as the Pillars of Hercules, only a day's sail away, were an inspiration:

'Beyond th'old Pillars many have travailed
Towards the Sun's cradle, and his throne, and bed;
A fitter Pillar our Earl did bestow
In that late Island; for he well did know
Farther than Wingfield no man dares to go.'[27]

The commanders attempted to protect churches from desecration, not always successfully. In the fever of iconoclasm inherited from Henry VIII's reign the soldiers tore the statue of the Virgin from the Jesuit church and dragged it through the streets to a bonfire.[28]

'27. Sunday in the afternoon the Lords General did knight these gentlemen whose names ensue:

Don Christophero Prince of Portugal
Robert Earl of Sussex
Count Ludovik of Nassau
William Lord Herbert
Richard Lord Burke
Sir William Howard
Sir George Devereux
Sir Henry Newell
Sir Edwin Riche
Sir [Space left blank] Lavins Netherlander
Sir [Space left blank] Aguemort Netherlander
Sir Antony Ashley
Sir Henry Leonard
Sir Richard Leveson
Sir Horatio Vere
Sir Arthur Throgmorton

Sir Miles Corbett
Sir Edward Conway
Sir Oliver Lambert
Sir Antony Cooke
Sir John Townsend
Sir Christopher Hayden
Sir Francis Popham
Sir Philip Woodhouse
Sir Alexander Clifford
Sir Maurice Berkeley
Sir Charles Blount
Sir George Gyfford
Sir Robert Cross
Sir James Scudamore
Sir Uryas Lee
Sir John Lee
Sir Richard Weston
Sir Richard Waynman
Sir James Wotton

Sir Richard Ruddall

Sir Thomas Ackton

Sir Robert Mansell

Sir Thomas Gates

Sir William Monson

Sir Gilly Merrick

Sir [John] Bolles

Sir Thomas Smyth

Sir Edward Bowes

Sir William Pooley

Sir Humphrey Drewell

Sir Thomas Palmer

Sir Amyas Preston

Sir John Stafford

Sir Robert Remington

Sir William Lovell

Sir John Buck

Sir John Gilbert

Sir John Morgan

Sir William Harvey

Sir John Alderidge

Sir Gerard Harvey

Sir John Shelton

Sir Alexander Radcliffe

Sir William Ashenden

Sir Robert Dudley.[29]

Sir Matthew Browne

'28. Monday. The Lords Generals knighted Sir William Harvey and towards evening at the Master of the Ordnance's lodging a consultation was held upon the former proposition, whether the town was fit to be held or no, having sufficient means to leave victuals to maintain 5,000 men for four months. By the Selected Council it was agreed that it was fit to be held because in that time sufficient means of supply might be made. The Lords Generals themselves in their own ships with the weakest of the fleet should return for England; the Lord Thomas Howard and Sir Walter Raleigh with forty of the best ships of war should go to the Islands to lie for the Indian fleet.

'To this consultation, when the Selected Council had delivered their opinions, the colonels of the Army were called in and made acquainted with this project, whereunto they were required to deliver their censures. By the general consent of them all, the former opinion was confirmed, but in conclusion the Lord General Essex, albeit he agreed in opinion with all the rest for the holding of the city, yet dissented from the same unless himself might be left in the guard of it, protesting that he would quit himself of all blame if harm or danger should, which he prophesied would, happen to the Army if himself were absent, but, if he might remain with the garrison, all harm and danger should light upon himself. His reasons were that his absence would be the cause of their ruin, for that his credit, he feared, would not be sufficient to send them supplies, whereas his presence would undoubtedly assure present success. This being by his Lordship protested, every man changed his opinion, and by general consent it was concluded that it was fit to abandon the town.'[30]

Why did the Council, which hitherto had been so united and firm in its conduct of the expedition, vacillate in such an extraordinary manner about what to do next? The idea of having a force sufficient to hold Cadiz had certainly been in the mind of Essex from the start; the dateline that Sir George Carew proudly wrote on his first letter home to Sir Robert Cecil, '30th June, from Her Majesty's city of Cadiz'[31] shows that he too favoured the project; and Sir Francis Vere had stated as early as March that not to hold Cadiz would make the campaign seem a mere 'summer's bravery'.[32] On the other hand Sir George and Sir Walter had more experience than the others of military operations at the far end of a long and vulnerable line of communication. Raleigh had lost his Virginia colonists partly because, owing to the imminence of the Armada, men, ships and supplies could not be spared for them. His cousin had seen men cut off and surrounded in the Irish wars. It seemed therefore, on reconsideration, that if Essex were not left in command of the occupation force, the Privy Council might not be persuaded to send out supplies. And would the ships be able to battle with the midwinter Atlantic and reach the garrison before their four months' stores were exhausted? Moreover, there was little chance of acquiring further loot by staying in Cadiz, and Essex had come to feel that, unless some further success were achieved, the Queen might not be satisfied with what only two days before had appeared a brilliant achievement. This presentiment grew daily in a mind already too volatile, and on the voyage home he wrote, with a punning reference to his familiar name of Robin, these melancholic lines:

'Happy were he could finish forth his fate
In some unhaunted desert, where, obscure
From all society, from love and hate
Of worldly folk, there should he sleep secure;
Then wake again, and yield God ever praise;

89

Content with hip, with haws, and brambleberry;
In contemplation passing still his days,
And change of holy thoughts to keep him merry;
Who, when he dies, his tomb might be the bush
Where harmless Robin resteth with the thrush:
    —Happy were he!'
'29. Tuesday. They continued in the town ransacking the base
pillage of all sorts.'[33]

A distinction was drawn between pillage, that is the picking up
of heterogeneous loose objects, and the seizure of treasure or
prizes. When the Cadiz accounts were rendered, 'a box of printed
books' was 'esteemed pillage and therefore not valued'. These may
have been the books on religion and philosophy brought home by
Edward Doughtie, a chaplain in *Ark Royal* who afterwards became
Dean of Hereford and left them to the Cathedral Library. One of
these is inscribed 'Edw: Doughtie *in expeditione Cadiz on 21 Junij
1596*'. Another, autographed by him, was given to Sir Thomas
Bodley for his library at Oxford.

The private soldier had different tastes. The Admiral's
physician noted that 'some of the baser sort', in plundering the
town, 'by the over-great plenty of wine, oil, almonds, olives,
raisins, spices and other rich groceries were knocked out and lay
trampled under foot in every common highway'.[34] Englishmen had
a shocking reputation in Europe for drunkenness, but according to
some Elizabethan writers, they had adopted their drinking habits
from the Dutch. Sir John Smythe, a veteran soldier, wrote:

'This foreign vice hath been brought out of those Low Countries
by some of our such men of war within these very few years,
whereof it is come to pass that nowadays there are very few feasts
where our said men of war are present but they do invite and
procure all the company, of what calling soever they be, to
carousing and quaffing. And because they will not be denied
their challenges, they will with many new congees, ceremonies
and reverences drink to the health and prosperity of princes, to
the health of counsellors, and unto the health of their greatest
friends both at home and abroad, in which exercise they never

cease till they be dead drunk, or as the Flemings say, *doot dronken.*'[35]

'30. Wednesday. After sunset the Lord General Essex, the Lord Marshal and most of the gentlemen of the Army with 29 companies of foot and one cornet of horse without sound of drum made head into the Island towards the bridge for no other end but to see what countenance the enemy did hold. About a mile short of the castle near to the bridge the Army made halt, and drew forth 300 foot somewhat nearer the castle to lie in ambuscado to cut off such as should sally forth of the castle. This night in Cadiz Sir George Carew, Master of the Ordnance, had the charge of the town, the Lord Admiral being aboard the ships.'[36]

It was a fearsome assignment. There was not a regiment in which discipline had not been loosened by drink and the excitement of selling or bartering each item of pillage. By this process every man could, with a modicum of honesty, say, if questions were asked about what he held, that everything had been legitimately acquired. Liquor made every haggle a potential cause for an affray. Sir George, a fellow citizen of Shakespeare, his wife having recently inherited Clopton House close by Stratford-on-Avon, may well have described the scene to the poet and lived to hear Othello address the captain of his guard:

'. . . Give me to know
How this foul rout began, who set it on:
And he that is approved in this offence,
Though he had twinn'd with me, both at a birth,
Shall lose me.—What, in a town of war,
Yet wild, the people's hearts brimful of fear,
To manage private and domestic quarrel,
In night, and on the court and guard of safety!
'Tis monstrous.'[37]

'July 1. Thursday morning by break of day certain loose soldiers were sent to burn houses close by the castle in hope to draw forth part of the guard within our ambuscado, but the enemy, either for fear or in discretion, made no sally. The Earl of Essex, being in the head of his cornet, which were about 60 lances, leaving his Army where they made halt, came within shot of the castle, giving them many bravados to procure them to a skirmish, but nothing could provoke them to skirmish or one to make a shot from the walls. Whereupon the Earl retreated to his forces and so to the town, and on the way gave the honour of knighthood to Mr. Gray.

'In this meantime the *Nonpareil*, the *Vanguard* and the *Rainbow*, the *Mary Rose* with other ships were commanded by the Lord Admiral to weigh, and to fight with the king's galleys which proudly came from Rota and came to the mouth of the Bay of Cadiz, but when our ships were come near them without entering shot, and certain pieces discharged which killed divers of their men, the wind being so bare as we could make no way, they fled, making all possible haste along the coast towards St. Lucar.

'After the return of the Lord General Essex to the town he gave the honour of knighthood to Captain Baldwin Merkyrk, Sergeant Major of his Regiment, and to Captain Gerard Harvey, being both wounded at the surprise of Cadiz.

'2. Friday. Being the uttermost day requested by the prisoners for the payment of the 120,000 ducats not being then come, the 50 prisoners that were in pledge for it were distributed amongst the ships.

'3. Saturday. The Lords stayed yet in Cadiz, expecting the payment of the 120,000 crowns aforesaid, but the money came not. 2 messengers only were sent from the Duke of Medina, one a canon of Cadiz, the other a gentleman of Xeres called Matteo, Marquis di Gaetano, to the Generals to entreat them to deliver the prisoners and to accept merchants' bills and bonds for the payment thereof which was by the Lords refused.[38]

'Captain Fishbourne, who was left at Plymouth by reason of the leak which was in the *Jonas*, came to us to Cadiz, bringing with him a caravel, and had aboard him Captain Collyer and his company.[39]

'4. Sunday morning. Order was given for the embarking of all the Army by regiments. The first that was shipped were the regiment of Sir Horatio Vere, who had Sir John Wingfield's regiment, and Sir Richard Wingfield, then the regiments of Sir

Conyers Clifford and Sir Thomas Gerrard, and after them the regiments of Sir Christopher Blount and the Earl of Sussex, and lastly the regiments of the Lord Marshal and the Lord General Essex, which two regiments were upon the guard of the port of the town to the landward until the rest were embarked, and of them all drawn away but 300, which were of his Lordship's regiment only, who stayed upon that guard to the last, and were shipped by the Lord General Essex himself, who, accompanied with divers great officers and sundry gentlemen of the Army, stayed to see the last men aboard. By that the two first regiments were embarked, the town was begun to be fired, which left not burning in our view until Wednesday night following, at which time we lost sight thereof. Moreover this night all the sick and hurt in the Army were selected from the rest and dispersed with ships appointed for that purpose to make their present return into England.'[40]

The embarkation was complicated by the quantity of loot which each man tried to take with him, so that Howard was forced to send a note to Essex:

'Where your Lordship doth write to have the sick men in their own ships, I think your meaning is that the soldiers shall all return in the ships they went out of, and so I have sent the boats to do, but you shall do well [to arrange that] officers may go with the sick men that may best order it, but you shall see that the luggage will pester the sick men, and that some will have more care of that than of the men. Divers boats yesterday and this night are come with luggage that might better have brought sick men. I send the boats with all speed, and God send you and your company well aboard and me some fresh meat.

The *Ark* 10 o'clock.'[41]

'[4] And further the Hollanders, riding furthest into the bay, sent certain companies ashore towards the castle fast by the bridge, at sight of whose approach the enemy abandoned the fort, and the Hollanders burnt it to the ground, as, that castle excepted, the whole Island was formerly burnt by the Lord General Essex on the Thursday before.'[42]

The Duke of Medina Sidonia received the news of all these

disasters with his customary fortitude.

'It is plainly,' he wrote, 'a chastisement from Our Lord and His will alone. Blessed be His Name, though the loss has been very great.'

His countrymen had been defeated on their own soil, and a Spanish officer, Don Luis Fajorde, reported to Philip II:

'It is not so much that in six hours we have lost so famous a city and port, with a fleet of war and a *flota* and the standard of Xeres and 600 horses, as the prestige that is destroyed, in this the enemy have seen that even in Andalusia, the most fertile and populous province in Spain, we could not in a fortnight gather forces enough about Cadiz to turn them out of the city, not to strike so much as a blow, while they enjoyed its spoil, and that of all the island and its territory, with as much security and pleasure as though they had been in the river of London. So that now here we stand watching the temples and homes of that miserable city in flames; and though we are so near that the smoke is driving in our eyes, we know, with what feelings your Majesty may imagine, that we cannot stir a finger to save it.'[43]

The best-informed ruler in Europe, the Doge of Venice, heard from Agustino Nani, ambassador to the court of Philip II, that 'the courier who brought his Majesty news of the English landing and what followed, arrived at Toledo while the King was reposing, and Don Christoforo de Mora would not wake him up to give him such bad news, delaying to communicate it till three hours after the courier's arrival, when his Majesty was dressed. When his Majesty learned this, he complained to Don Christoforo of the delay, but showed a Christian fortitude in bearing the blow. And although overcome by the news, yet it seemed to lend him vigour, for he rose from his chair and walked a few paces, a thing which the weakness of his legs and the remains of the gout had not hitherto allowed him to do, and straightway, without any signs of a perplexed mind, he began to issue numerous orders and to make various provisions . . .'[44]

Sir George Carew agreed with Don Luis Fajorde's assessment:

'[4] In all this time of our being in Cadiz, which was 14 days, albeit the enemy was gathered to a head at Seville, Xeres, Port St. Mary [and] Port Real to an army of about 50,000 strong, yet in this time we never had alarm either by land or sea to disturb, but lived in as great tranquillity and ease as if we had been in Cheapside.'[45]

## Chapter IV Notes

1. Duke of Northumberland's MS.
2. Documentos Ineditos de Espana, Simancas.
3. Lambeth Codex 250.
4. On board *Mere Honour* the Lord Admiral laid guns with his own hands 'and so bestowed his shot upon the galleys' that they left the scene altogether. (Harleian 167.)
5. Ragusans—ships from Ragusa (now Dubrovnik) a port on the Dalmatian coast of the Adriatic.
6. This flyboat belonged to the Dutch squadron. Her Captain-Lieutenant, his two sons and forty-eight of her crew were killed; only her Captain-Pilot and twenty men were saved.
    The Englishmen were saved by the Dutch, who also attempted to board the *St. Philippo* and seize her flag as evidence that she was their prize. (Kaiserl. Bibliothek Wien, Cod. MS. 13,033 Suppl. 383 f.34a–39a.)
7. Lambeth Codex 250.
8. John Donne, *A Burnt Ship*, Epigrams.
9. Lambeth Codex 250.
10. *An English Garner*, Vol. VII, 1883.
11. Duke of Northumberland's MS.
12. 'Freely' indicates that no ransom was being asked. When it is not used, the implication is that some unspecified arrangement, exchange or ransom, had been made.
13. The Dutch claim that before the English landed, Jan Garbrandsz, Vice-Admiral of the Hollanders, went ashore with fourteen men and took Puntal, from which the garrison had fled, even though there were four cannon on it, and was thus the first to set foot on land and to raise the flag of the Prince of Orange. (Kaiserl. Bibliothek Wien, Cod. MS. 13,033 Suppl. 383 f.34a–39a).
14. The Queen's commission to the commanders automatically entitled them to confer knighthoods in the field. The only cause for contemporary comment was the large number. (See Note 29 below.)
15. Lambeth Codex 250.
16. Hatfield 44.18.
17. Duke of Northumberland's MS.

18. Hatfield 139.59.
19. Don Guzman, the Duke of Medina Sidonia, a man of great courage and integrity, had commanded the 1588 Armada. Members of his family had for centuries held important posts in Church and State and his estates extended over a vast area of western Andalusia, where he owned corn lands, vineyards, orange groves and tunny fisheries. He was responsible for, among other things, coastal defence, and may have given orders that the Indies fleet should be burnt. On the other hand a document in his family archives states that the orders were given by Don Francisco Tello and the General Luis Alfonso Flores.
20. Lambeth Codex 250.
21. Hatfield 39.43/44. 'The Cardinal' is the Archduke Albrecht, Viceroy of the Netherlands.
22. Lambeth Codex 250.
23. Lambeth Codex 250.
24. Harleian 167.
25. Lambeth Codex 250.
26. Edward Maria Wingfield, a Catholic merchant, godson of Mary Queen of Scots, sailed with Captain John Smith to Virginia nine years later.
27. John Donne, *Sir John Wingfield*, Epigrams.
28. This statue was only partially burnt. The English Catholic students then in college at Valladolid petitioned to be allowed to have it and to atone for the violence of their countrymen by placing it above the high altar in their chapel. Their request was granted, and it remains there to this day.
29. The story was told of Sir John Bolles that one of the Spanish ladies taken prisoner in the town fell in love with him and asked not be released, but to be taken to England. He explained that he was married, but, before parting, she gave him a gold chain and a picture of herself in a green dress, together with jewels and plate as presents for his wife. The portrait hung in the Bolles' family home, Thorpe Hall in Lincolnshire, for many years. The families of other knights of Cadiz, Sir Richard Leveson, Sir Francis Popham and Sir Uryas Lee also claim that each was wooed in this way by a captured Spanish lady. A ballad, *The Spanish Lady's Love*, became very popular and was parodied in Rowley's *A Match at Midnight* in 1633.
    It was generally believed that the knights of Cadiz came home with little but honour for their pains:
    'A gentleman of Wales and a knight of Cales,
    And a laird of the North Countrie,
    A Yeoman of Kent with his yearly rent
    Could buy them out all three.'

30. Lambeth Codex 250.
31. Hatfield 41.99.
32. Hatfield 30.109.
33. Lambeth Codex 250.
34. Harleian 167.
35. *Instructions, Observations and Orders Militarie requisite for all Chieftaines, Captains and higher and lower men of charge and officers to understand know and observe Composed by Sir John Smythe, 1591, and now first imprinted 1594 London by Richard Jones.*
36. Lambeth Codex 250.
37. Shakespeare, *Othello* II iii 206–14.
38. The Lord Admiral wrote in Latin to the Duke of Medina Sidonia, 'thinking himself not wholly unknown' to him, and expressing the wish that thirty-one English subjects serving in the galleys should be released. In return he promised to hand over an equal number of Spanish prisoners, though they were of higher rank. (Hatfield 41.98.)
39. The Admiral had been unable to find a substitute for the *Jonas* on 3 June.
40. Lambeth Codex 250.
41. Hatfield 47.101.
42. Lambeth Codex 250.
43. Documentos Ineditos de Espana, Simanacas.
44. State Papers Venetian 1596.
45. Sir George Carew's London house was in Cheapside. He dates two letters to Lord Burghley from it in 1593. (State Papers Ireland 1593.)

# V

# No enemy
# to make resistance

'[4] This night we weighed anchor and upon boards freed ourselves out of the bay into the road, where we anchored.

'5. Monday. In the afternoon a galley was sent from Don Juan de Puertocarrero, who brought letters from him and the Marquis St. Croce to the Lord Admiral with 39 English captains for exchange of so many of their nation, which was assented unto, and accordingly exchange made. The rest of the English captains at Seville and St. Lucar were likewise promised to be sent forthwith upon like conditions.'[1]

Donne was shocked by the sight of these men and imagined that, but for the fortune of war, he might have been captured and suffered as they had done:

'. . . When weather-beaten I come back; my hand,
Perhaps with rude oares torn, or sun beams tann'd.
My face and breast of haircloth, and my head
With cares rash sudden stormes, being o'rspread,
My body a sack of bones, broken within,
And powder's blue stains scatter'd on my skin: . . .'[2]

The unfortunate prisoners taken from Drake's force in the Caribbean did not reach Seville in time to be included.

'[5] This galley in her coming into our fleet, being then under sail over against Rota, from whence she carried so small a flag of truce as it could hardly be discerned, was shot at by one of our small barks and killed two or three men.

'6. Tuesday. The wind so bare as we did not pass Rota 2 leagues from Cadiz.

'7. Wednesday. About 10 a clock athwart of Chipiona 2 flyboats, bound for Cadiz and laden with deal boards, as far as is yet known, fell in to our fleet, whereof the one was taken, and the other by the goodness of his sail got into the Bar of St. Lucar.

'8. Thursday. Calms and bare winds so as all the day we gained little in our course.

'9. Friday. The Generals met aboard the *Ark*, where it was agreed that we should land our forces at Ayamonte, from thence to pass over the water to Castro Marim then to march to Tavira, and so to Faro. Also the same day Sir Antony Ashley in the *Lion's Whelp* was dispatched to the court of England, and for that the Earl of Sussex was fallen sick, which proved of the measles, and desirous to return for England, Sir Robert Cross in the *Swiftsure* was commanded to transport him. Also with these ships Sir Gilly Merrick, and about 14 sail more of hoys, flyboats and small barks with horses, sick men and pillage had licence to depart. Upon whose departure the Master of the Ordnance in the *Mary Rose* did bear the Vice-Admiral's flag of that Squadron.

'10. Saturday morning the Generals, for fear of being embayed within the Cape of St. Marie, if any thing were attempted at Ayamonte, which is to the east of the said cape about 8 leagues, they altered their purpose and resolved to land and water at Faro, a city in the Algarve and the chief port in it, in which town there is ever resident a Bishop.

'11. Sunday morning before sun rising a seaboard our fleet eleven of the king's galleys gave chase to a flyboat called the *Peter* of Enkuizen, bound for England and to a small [man] of Plymouth appertaining to Sir Ferdinando Gorges, which two ships were of our Army. The *Peter* of Enkuizen within a league ahead of our fleet was taken by the galleys and towed away, being impossible to rescue her by reason of the dead calm. But the small man of Plymouth escaped, they being afraid to spend longer time in the which our ships might come up to them. In this flyboat we lost of hurt and sick soldiers and mariners, English and Flemish, about 120 persons and sundry horses appertaining to the Lord Thomas Howard, the Master of the Ordnance etc. and some pillage of good value.

'12. Monday morning. The Lord Thomas Howard with about 40 sail in his company, whom we had lost 4 days before, was descried to stern of us to the eastward, who before night came into our fleet. Also this day Sir Baldwin Merkyrk, Sergeant Major of the Lord General Essex' regiment, who was hurt as aforesaid at the winning of Cadiz, died of his wound, and was buried in sea close along the shore a little to the westward of the Cape St. Marie. And towards night, having a stiff gale of wind from the shore, we bore room into the sea.

'13. Tuesday morning we made into land, and before ten a clock the whole fleet came to anchor before the mouth of the westerly creek of the haven of Faro, and with all possible expedition both the Lords Generals and the whole Army were disembarked and landed upon the point of land opposite to the Island whose easterly point is the Cape St. Marie. The heat of the day being very extreme, the Lord Admiral, whose years and body [were] unfit for travail, and especially in the hot climate, was so distempered with the heat as by the entreaty of the Lord General Essex and others, contrary to his desires, returned to his ships. After sun setting the whole Army began to march, and encamped about a good mile into the country.

'14. Wednesday. At the discharging of the watch the vanguard, led by Sir Christopher Blount, whose regiment had the point, began to march. The whole Army followed, ranging into 18 battalions. The Earl himself, finding the gentlemen adventurers whose names ensue, ranged in the front of the vanguard, left his horse and led the same himself, on whom, besides the Colonel and Captains of the Regiment, the Prince of Portugal, the Lord Thomas Howard and the Master of the Ordnance attended. In the march we saw no enemy to make resistance, and all that we saw were few horse and foot scattered upon hills to view our troops. About 12 a clock the vanguard entered into the city of Faro, being distant from our landing above three leagues, where the inhabitants were fled with their goods, insomuchas hardly any person could be found and the houses left bare and naked. The Lord General quartered himself in the Bishop's house.

'The names of these gentlemen adventurers that bore pikes and marched in the front of the vanguard, led by the Lord General:

[a page was left blank but the names were never entered].'³

That night Essex selected 178 books from the Bishop's library, mostly works on religion, canon law and scholastic philosophy, together with one manuscript and next morning had them carried down to the ships. Many were large volumes magnificently bound and bore in gold the family coat-of-arms of Ferdinand Martins Mascarenhas, the Grand Inquisitor of Portugal, who had been Rector of Coimbra University before being ordained bishop of Faro in 1594. He was a great scholar and had bought books from all over western Europe, a number of them newly published. The manuscript, a life of St. John the Baptist in Portuguese, had been dedicated to him. Against those who had robbed him he raged in Ciceronian style: *'Hostes impii, insolentes, superbi, truculenti, iracundi . . . piratae non minus ab humanitate quam a religione abhorrentes'* (Impious foes, insolent, arrogant, quarrelsome, outrageous . . . pirates who abhor humanity no less than religion).[4] As a bibliophile Essex was his equal, and, rejecting all offers to ransom the books, eventually gave them to Sir Thomas Bodley, who was forming the nucleus of the famous Oxford University library that bears his name. There they still remain, gracing the room where Duke Humphrey's medieval manuscripts were housed before the Protestant reformers dispersed them as being papist and worthless.

'15. Thursday. By break of day the Master of the Ordnance his company, by order from the Lord General one way and Captain Sir Clement Heigham, Captain Brett and Captain Upsher, with certain troops compounded of all the companies to the number of six hundred, marched another way into the country towards the mountains, and before night all returned, having burnt many villages and houses, with cattle and other good pillage. In this march divers of our men with drunkenness, faintness and scattering were cut off by the enemy, who ever more were in sight, but never durst charge the troops. Also the same day Don Juan de Puertocarrero wrote unto the Lord Admiral for the releasing of Don Diego Cabezza de Vacca, prisoner of Sir Baldwin Merkyrk deceased.[5]

'The galleys by him sent with this message, who came with a flag of truce, came to anchor in the middle of the Island of the

Cape St. Marie between our fleet, which were at anchor at either end of the island that leads to Faro, but upon the admonition of the Lord Admiral, because they were on his safe conduct, they quitted their anchorage and made out into the sea. By these messengers we had intelligence that the *Peter* of Enkuizen, which was taken the Sunday afore, as aforesaid, before such time as she had yielded, lost 30 of her own company and slew 40 of the enemy by a train of powder that blew them up when they were entered.

'16. Friday. By mischance a Dutch Captain, and of good estimation amongst them, was by a soldier of Captain Talkerns in the market slain with the blow of musket, for which fact by the marshal's court he was adjudged to be shot to death,[6] upon whom about four a clock, the whole Army being in the market place, execution was done, and immediately the vanguard marched towards the water side, and before four a clock the rearguard, led by the Lord General himself, was drawn forth, leaving the town burnt to the ground.[7] This night we encamped again where we lodged after our landing.

'17. Saturday. Before 4 a clock in the afternoon the whole Army was embarked again. Which done, the Generals and Selected Council met aboard the *Ark*, where a consultation was held what was fit to be done by our Army before our return into England, where every man's opinion was demanded and heard, but nothing concluded, but referred to a second meeting.

'18. Sunday morning the Lords Generals and Council met aboard the *Repulse* where, after large debating, it was agreed that the whole fleet should not make stay or water in any place until we come to the Rock in the mouth of the river of Lisbon, and there to consider what further should be done. Which done, having a leading wind, we set sail.

'19. Monday. Continued our course for Cape St. Vincent, the wind not being very large.

'20. Tuesday. About one a clock in the afternoon we doubled the Cape St. Vincent, within saker[8] shot of the shore with a frank wind at the last, but we had not sailed four leagues to the northward of the Cape but we met with the land breeze, which did over blow and carried us into the sea.

'21. 22. Wednesday and Thursday. Dry and stormy, continuing constantly at north.

'23. Friday. Towards the afternoon the storm was fully spent and the Lords Generals aboard the *Ark* hung forth a flag of the Queen's Arms, whereupon the Selected Council met, where it was concluded that we should make for the Island of St. Michael in the Azores, where a good hope was left either to meet with the East Indian or West Indian fleet, assured means of water, whereof the fleet had great want, and the Island in itself rich, but if we should happily meet with a strong westerly wind insomuchas upon no board we could recover the Islands, then the purpose was to go for England. At this Council was likewise dispatched into England the *Centurion*, the *Elizabeth*, the *Gift of God*, the *George* of London, the *Jacob* of Rotterdam, the *Peter*, and the *Jacob* of Enkuizen with certain hoys of horses.

'24. Saturday. The wind came about to the west, and west south-west, insomuchas with that wind there was no course to hold to the Islands, whereupon these ships, formerly dismissed for England, were stayed, and the fleet bore to the northwards, in which course, by reason of foul weather, the fleet was wonderfully scattered.

'25. Sunday. The stiff gale continued, in the which the fleet gathered together again.

'26. Monday morning. A flag of the Queen's Arms was hung forth of the *Ark*, whereupon the Council assembled. The questions debated was to understand whether it was more fit to lie for the return of the carracks, or to direct our course for England, the opinion of the major part, if a competent fleet victualled might be selected out of the navy, that it were fit to lie off and on upon the height of the Rock until the return of the carracks, but finding an impossibility to raise such a fleet as aforesaid, it was concluded by the general assent of all, that we should stand for the Northerly Cape, called Cape Finisterre, and then to put in for the Groyne, if upon discovery it should be found that any ships of the king's were in that harbour.'⁹

The harbour called the Groyne or La Corunna lay at the head of a semi-circular inlet two miles wide and three miles deep in the extreme north-west of Spain. Open to the north and protected from the Atlantic swell coming in from the west by a low rocky promontory only half a mile wide, it was not a harbour that sailing vessels found easy to enter or leave. Pilots recommended outgoing vessels to sail early in the morning when the wind normally blew off the land, so avoiding breezes from the sea later in the day. The old town lay on a small spur of land jutting out into the harbour.

'27. Tuesday. The day fair, little wind, but that which was, fit for our course. After sun set a stiff gale arose from west south-west which continued all that night.

'28. Wednesday. Towards the evening a storm of wind and rain arose, in the which the Earl of Essex, having the *Warspite*, the *Vanguard* with other ships not exceeding 20 sail in his company, continuing their course, lost the Lord Admiral and the rest of the fleet, who immediately upon the setting of the sun tacked about and bare room into the sea.

'29. Thursday. The day calmy and fair.

'30. Friday morning about 8 upon a starboard bow we made the North Cape, commonly called Cape Finisterre, and before ten a clock far off under our lee, near to the shore, we descried the Earl with the ships which were on Wednesday lost. Towards night, because we were not able to double the Cape on that board, the whole fleet bare room into the sea. This evening the Lord General with his ships fell into the fleet.

'31. Saturday. The day fair, the wind large, insomuchas before night we had doubled the Northerly Cape and were athwart Monicy. This day West, master[10] of the *Mary Rose*, by the Lord Admiral's direction, was sent in a caravel to discover what shipping rode within the harbour at the Groyne.

'August 1. Sunday morning by 8 a clock we came before the entrance of the haven of the Groyne, where the caravel dispatched the day before returned unto us with the report that in those harbours there was no shipping. Whereupon a flag of Council was hung forth and the Lords and Council met aboard the *Ark*, where it was resolved we should forthwith direct our course for England, upon consideration that there was not, in the Groyne or far off at that present, any shipping, and also in regard there was great want of victuals in the fleet, insomuchas the most were not victualled for above 14 days, as the weak[ness] of estate the fleet was in by reason of sickness.'[11]

The Venetian Ambassador in Madrid wrote to the Doge: 'It is commonly reported that the English fleet has gone back to England because it is suffering from a very bad epidemic of spotted fever.'[12] This was almost certainly measles.

'[1] This day aboard the *Ark* the Admiral of Holland, called Sir John van Duivenvoorde, did receive by the Lords Generals jointly the honour of knighthood.

'Also Sir Walter Raleigh, in regard of the great sickness that was aboard his ship, obtained leave to make the best haste he could to Plymouth. With him there were dispatched, with letters to the Queen and the Council from the Lords Generals, Sir Arthur Savage, Sir Edward Conway and Master George Buck. Buck was dispatched with the report that our purpose was to go for the Islands, and there to attend the carracks and bare date the [space left blank] July. Sir Arthur Savage was dispatched with our purpose to leave the course towards the Islands and to make for the Groyne and bare date the [space left blank] of July. Sir Edward Conway was to make relation what we found at the Groyne, and our purpose to make for England, as also to know Her Majesty's pleasure, what her will is should be done with this Army, whether it shall be cashiered or no. With Sir Walter Raleigh the *Roebuck* and the *John and Francis* were dismissed.

'2. Monday. The *Affection* and *St. Thomas*, Master Watts' ships, being victualled with a proportion above the rest of the fleet, obtained leave of the Lords Generals to return for the Cape with purpose to lie off and on to spend the remainder of the provisions in hope to get purchase. All the day calms.

'3. Tuesday and Monday. Calmy.

'4. Wednesday. The wind came good and blew in a stiff gale westerly whereby, by the storm and by their desires homeward, everyone taking his own course, the fleet was dispersed and scattered.

'5. Thursday. The wind good, and they held on their courses for England.

'6. Friday. The Lord Thomas Howard and Sir Walter Raleigh came into the Sound of Plymouth, the *Mere Honour* being in great danger to have been sunk by the abundance of water which was in by reason of a leak which by no means they could stop, nor hardly by pumping preserve from sinking.'[13]

The leaky state of *Mere Honour* was not regarded as extraordinary. Very few ships, whether large or small, were dry, the reason being that no technical method was known for so fitting the timbers together that they could not work apart in heavy weather. The traditional means of caulking seams was to ram in oakum (loose fibres of old hempen rope that had been teased out). Even good ships like the *Ark Royal* suffered occasionally from bad workmanship. In February 1588 the Lord Admiral had been full of praise for her, but five weeks later reported: 'The *Ark* is arrived this morning here at Margate, wonderfully well trimmed and mended of her leak, which was a bolt forgotten to be driven in, and the outside covered with pitch, so it could not be seen; and when the sea had washed it off, then brake in the leak; and she was not well caulked in any place, but now most perfect.'[14]

'7. Saturday. The Lord Admiral with the gross of the fleet came into the Sound of Plymouth, which day the Earl of Essex in the *Repulse*, Sir George Carew in the *Mary Rose*, the Flemish squadron and the remainder of the fleet made the Lizard,[15] being the first part of England that was discovered.

'8. Sunday. The Lord General Essex with the rest came into the Sound of Plymouth, being that day ten weeks of the Lords' shipping there at Plymouth.'[16]

*Chapter V Notes*

1. Lambeth Codex 250.
2. John Donne, *His Picture*, Elegie V.
3. Lambeth Codex 250.
4. Mascarenhas, *De Auxiliis Divinae Gratiae*.
5. The medieval orders of chivalry laid down that if a knight captured a foe in battle and held him to ransom, but died before receiving payment, the captive should be allowed to go free.
6. This was in accordance with the instructions issued at Plymouth

forbidding any man to strike an officer on pain of death—see Chapter II (Duke of Northumberland's MS.).

7. It is surprising that the Portuguese prince, Don Christophero, should have agreed to this terrible act, which cannot have improved his brother Don Emanuel's chances of succession to the throne.

8. A saker was a small cannon with a range of about half a mile.

9. Lambeth Codex 250.

10. The master was responsible for handling the ship and keeping her on course as directed by the captain, who was in over-all command. The presence of a master does not indicate that the captain lacked a knowledge of seamanship.

11. Lambeth Codex 250.

12. State Papers Venetian 1596.

13. Lambeth Codex 250.

14. State Papers Domestic 1588.

15. Sir William Monson in his *Tracts* vividly described the hazards of the western approaches, and argued in favour of building a lighthouse on the Lizard:

'If it be danger to haul in with the Lizard because of Scilly and the Gulf (Wolf Rock), as perhaps some will allege, I say that like danger is in hauling in with the Bolt, in respect of the Eddystone, that lieth more dangerously than the Gulf because it lieth in the course.

'But suppose a man does haul eight leagues to the westward or eastward at the Lizard, he shall have sight of the light and know certainly where he is. So that if he should be mistaken sixteen leagues in his reckoning he shall be helped by the view of the light.

'If it happen that a man fall between Scilly and the Land's End with a southerly wind, or in the night, or in a fog that they cannot descry land, if they escape the Gulf, which, as I have said, is no more dangerous than the Eddystone, they shall be more safer than hauling in with the shore as high as the Bolt, for they shall have sea room, and know certainly where they are by their sounding, for that side only affords ooze. As hauling betwixt the Lizard and the Bolt with a southerly wind, which is an embaying wind and commonly brings fogs and storms, a man shall be in danger to be put to the shore; therefore it may appear it is more safety to seek the Lizard, if a light be placed upon it, than to seek further into the Channel having no help but only art to help them.'

16. Lambeth Codex 250.

# VI

# Her Majesty's pleasure

The Queen's elation on first reading the dispatches that Sir Antony Ashley brought back from Cadiz was reflected in the stately rhetoric of her letter of greeting to the Lords Generals immediately after their return:

> 'You have made me famous, dreadful and renowned, not more for your victory than for your courage, nor more for either than for such plentiful liquor of mercy. Never was heard in so few days of so great a work achieved. Let the army know I care not so much for being Queen as that I am sovereign of such subjects.'[1]

Essex was the hero of the hour, and Edmund Spenser, responding to the public mood, included in his *Prothalamion* for the double wedding of Lady Elizabeth and Lady Katherine Somerset, daughters of the Earl of Worcester, praise no less extravagant than that expressed by the Queen herself:

> '. . . noble Peer,
> Great England's glory and the world's wide wonder,
> Whose dreadful name late through all Spain did thunder,
> And Hercules' two pillars standing near
> Did make to quake and fear.
> Fair branch of Honour, flower of Chivalry,
> That fillest England with thy triumph's fame,
> Joy have thou of thy noble victory!'

The Archbishop of Canterbury wrote to the bishops asking that thanksgiving services should be held in every church in the land. Before this could be organised, the unhappy man had instructions from the Queen; exercising her right as Supreme Governor of the Church, she ordered that only one Thanksgiving should be held—in St. Paul's. What had caused this change of mind? There

108

was nothing in the dispatches to justify it. Before the Selected Council took its final decision, the commanders had reached the unanimous conclusion that to return home was the only prudent course. Essex was in no way to blame, yet, when he arrived at court, he was not even given a private audience. Elizabeth usually received him informally and with every sign of affection; now, within the hearing of all, she declared angrily that, though she had spent £50,000 on equipping the expedition, it seemed that she was to receive no profit on her outlay. She even pretended to have been opposed to the expedition from the beginning, forgetting that at her command public prayers had been offered for its success. Her displeasure also had a deeper cause, offended vanity. She had long enjoyed living 'in that fierce light that beats upon a throne', and was disconcerted to find that for once all eyes were not upon her. Essex, his worst fears confirmed, realised that he would never be able to please his Sovereign; with age her temper had become too unpredictable, and in a sad letter to his friend Anthony Bacon, brother of the famous Francis, he wrote: 'I see the fruits of these kinds of employments, and, I assure you, I am as much distasted with the glorious greatness of a favourite as I was before with the supposed happiness of a courtier.'[2]

The Cecils, who could not resist any opportunity to discredit the Earl, whom they regarded as a dangerous rival, and no true friend of the Queen, set on foot a great many enquiries. A memorandum, corrected by Sir Robert, states that there was at Cadiz a Munition House worth 400,000 crowns, for which Sir George Carew and Sir Matthew Morgan must answer; a Custom House worth as much, for which Sir George and Sir John Aldridge must answer, and a Sugar House not inferior in value.

The scene at the Custom House was vividly described by Thomas Parre in a signed statement given to his interrogators:

'I say that, the day after the town was taken, I saw a great multitude of soldiers and mariners in the custom house, and Sir John Aldridge [Captain of Essex' horse], beating them forth. I endeavoured to assist him, but being too weak, he sent me to the Earl of Essex, Lord General, to inform him how they sought to ransack the place; whereupon Sir George Carew was sent with me to put back the ransackers, and I was left there with some of Sir George's men. Sir Richard Wingfield put another guard both in the house and at the doors, and the next day, a company of foot was quartered there, who dispossessed me. I saw packs of paper, chests of red caps, and glass; if anything else was there, it was ransacked before I arrived.'[3]

Sir Arthur Savage, who had been with Sir George on the first night of the occupation, also described what happened on 21 June: 'I was sent, late in the afternoon by the Lords Generals into the castle, with my Lord Essex' company of foot, of which I was lieutenant, to see no violence or wrong offered by the soldiers or other to any of the gentlewomen or the rest.'[4]

His men had been forbidden to enter any house, and remained on duty at the castle until 9 p.m. He then asked to be allotted a house belonging to a physician, where he might have his wounds attended to and take a night's rest. On his way there he met Sir George looking for his page, who was to direct him to a lodging. At Sir Arthur's invitation Sir George went to the physician's house and, while they were at supper, Sir George was sent for to take possession of treasure found nearby. This was one of the many duties laid upon the Master of the Ordnance at the start of the campaign.[5] Sir Arthur, asked to accompany him, replied that he had not slept for two days and two nights and must lie down. He was still asleep at dawn, when Sir George woke him to say what treasure had been found. Both men then went to sleep for two hours before going out to settle the matter. 'The most that was ever named to be there was 44,000 ducats', Sir Arthur concluded.[6]

That senior commanders, dropping with fatigue in the aftermath of battle, should actually have attempted to collect and list captured coin and treasure is extraordinary, yet Essex managed, with the aid of men like Carew, Savage and his own picked company, to maintain what was, by the standards of the time, excellent discipline.

Sir Matthew Morgan, Lieutenant Colonel of Essex's regiment, asked on his return that the Lords Generals should make 'some requital' and they bestowed on him 'the third part of the bells of Cadiz'. He had bought the other two thirds from Sir William Woodhouse and Mr. Trevor, together with four chests of red caps from Captain Henry Carew, a chain from a soldier for £14.10s.0d. and from Lieutenant Baynard a crystal bracelet set in gold for £4. 'Captain William Morgan,' he added, 'gave me an emerald worth £5; and part of a chain worth 40 marks was given to my lieutenant for a prisoner. I had three butts of Spanish wine, a hogshead of vinegar, a butt of wheat, and other things not worth the valuing. By my asking, travail and traffic, I hope I have made myself worth some £400 to £500.'[7]

Sir Gilly Merrick, a captain in Sir Conyers Clifford's regiment and a particular friend of Essex, came home with a formidable list of acquisitions, according to Sir Antony Ashley, including Barbary hides; sugars; a chest of plate with a hatful of pearls and amber at the bottom; velvets and silks; and sacks of coin taken from two captured Dutch flyboats.[8]

In Plymouth, the Privy Council heard, a great quantity of goods taken on the voyage had been offered for sale and fetched a high value 'to the defrauding of Her Majesty'.[9] Sir John Gilbert, Sir Ferdinando Gorges and other gentlemen were appointed Commissioners with the task of recovering them or their cash equivalent. At the same time in London the Queen appointed Alderman Billingsley, Mr. Carmarthen and Mr. Middleton to recover goods that had been brought into the Thames by captains, soldiers and mariners 'who pretend that they have had divers things given them by Lords Generals which were taken in the spoil of Cadiz'.[10] Her Majesty's intention was 'not to take from any man any things that ought to be allowed for lawful pillage, as apparel, household stuff, small pieces of plate and other such things', only money, jewels, gross stuff, plate and all manner of merchandise that 'ought to be preserved to defray the cost of the voyage'.[11] She received a report and valuation that there had been goods to a total value of £2,959.8s.8d. 'out of which £1,299.18s.0d. was secreted by the masters and mariners of 15 English ships'. At Bristol 'the *Mary Fortune* and the *Unicorn* that were in the late voyage, the one of them belonging to John Hopkins of that city, arriving lately in those parts, the Customer and other officers of that port, thinking to have made search in these vessels, were disappointed by the lewd behaviour of one Thomas Parre, captain, and Andrew Batten, master of the *Unicorn* and his mate with others, who presently the first night that they came into the road and the next morning fell to rummaging[12] the said ship and with small boats discharged various chests and trunks laden with goods of great value'. The unfortunate Mayor and his officers, Edward Gorges and George Snigg, were charged with the task of recovering the goods, examining the mariners' chests and returning to them only 'lawful pillage', a process they resisted 'in a disobedient manner' and with threats of violence.[13]

The Mayor of Southampton, Paul Elliott, with Sir Thomas West as his fellow commissioner, had an easier task than the Mayor of Bristol. The *Elizabeth* of Hampton landed two great chests and two packs of arras hangings and they were conveyed to the house of Sir Oliver Lambert, who willingly showed the contents to the Mayor. 'In the black barred chest', the clerks noted, were two whole pieces of Indian stuff like cloth of gold, four pieces of the same made in hangings, three pieces of hangings of branched silk, a bed of crimson taffeta, a green silk quilt etc. 'In the great barred chest', a petticoat of purple silk and gold embroidered with silver, nine crimson velvet cushions etc.[14]

Sir Francis Vere with his veterans returned to Holland immediately, taking their loot with them. The Lieutenant of Dover Castle, Thomas Fane, sent the port's chief searcher with some of the castle garrison to examine the cargoes of all the ships returning to the Netherlands, but when he arrived they were all setting sail, so that nothing could be done. 'I am credibly informed,' Fane wrote to Sir Robert Cecil, 'by men expert in such searches, it is not possible to make search in any ship to any good purpose, except the ship may first be cleared of all mariners and company therein, a matter not feasible in this instance.'[15] For Vere's men this was a second fortunate escape. At Plymouth he had been forced to defend them against sailors who had been confined to their ships when the soldiers were sacking Cadiz, and argued that they had not been given a fair share of the plunder. Sir Francis replied that the soldiers had risked their lives and deserved what they got; he probably suspected that the sailors, having loaded every package that the soldiers sent out from the shore, had charged quite enough for their services.

The Admiral of Holland received a handsome letter of thanks from the Queen, but his men went home discontented. They knew that on the two Dutch merchant ships taken off Cape St. Vincent

12. Title page of the works of St Gregory of Nyssa bearing inscription 'Edw: Doughtie, in expeditione Cadiz on 21 Junij 1596'. (*Hereford Cathedral Library, shelf-mark H.8.vi, by permission of The Dean and Chapter of Hereford Cathedral.*)

Casa blanca

The opening & appearing of the land or Mountaines
of Gibralter when you beginn to sayle into the Straight

S. Iuan del huerta

Condado grande

Moguer

Pielos

The Cliff

Salies

Salt pannes

Las arenas gordas
Redd Downes

Higuera

THE SEA COASTES
of Andaluzia made
according vnto the
right situation thereof
eauen as they appeare
& open with their
Riuers and
hauens .

MARIS OCCEAN

English
Spanish
Dutch
Ryth

13. Coast of Andalusia, showing harbour and island of Cadiz,
from Sir Antony Ashley's *The Mariner's Mirrour*, 1588.
(*Published by permission of the British Library*)

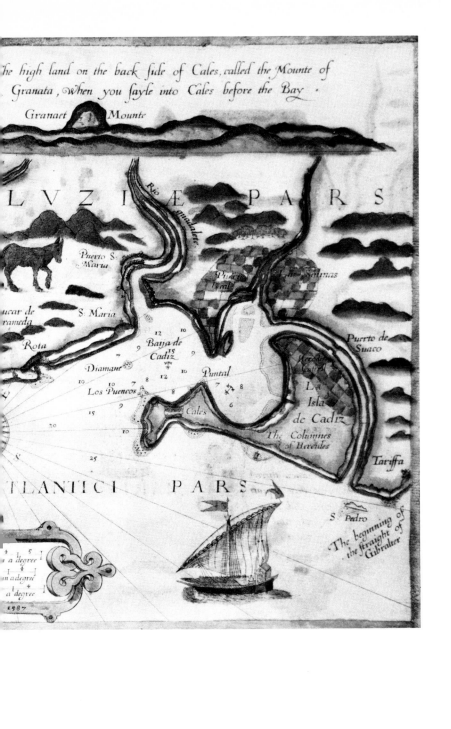

The high land on the back side of Cales, called the Mounte of
Granata, When you sayle into Cales before the Bay.

Granaet        Mounte

L V Z I Æ       P A R S

Rio guadalaier

Puerto S.
Maria

ucar de
rameda          S. Maria

Rota

Puerto de
Suaco

Baija de
Cadiz

Diamant

Los Puencos          Puntal

Cales

La
Isla
de Cadiz

The Colúmnes
of Hercúles

Tariffa

T L A N T I C I       P A R S

S. Pedro

The beginning of
the straight of
Gibralter

a degree
a degree
a degree

1587

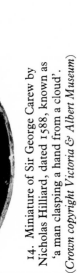

15. Head of Philip II on a
Netherlands Filipidaalder dated 1589,
from George III's collection, given to
the British Museum by George IV.
*(Reproduced by courtesy of the
Trustees of the British Museum)*

14. Miniature of Sir George Carew by
Nicholas Hilliard, dated 1588, known as
'a man clasping a hand from a cloud'.
*(Crown copyright Victoria & Albert Museum)*

there had been the colossal sum of 370,000 guilders, which the English should have handed over, seeing that it was money destined for Holland in payment for goods bought there. It was never returned. The Dutch also complained that, when the order to withdraw was given, the English had held the gates of Cadiz and robbed them of almost all their booty; what remained was seized on their return by the Dutch authorities, whose searchers were much better organised than their English counterparts. Moreover, no amends were made to those Dutch masters whose ships had been commandeered by the English and used as transports. In spite of all this, the Admiral remained a valuable friend of the English. He had argued strongly in favour of leaving a garrison in Cadiz and had stood by ready to give Essex's leaking ship aid when, nearing Plymouth, she had been in danger.[16]

Sir Antony Ashley, who shared with Sir George responsibility for registering the amount of treasure and coin taken, was held at the Fleet prison in London for weeks and harassed with a stream of hostile questions about what happened on the first night of the occupation: Was the door of the low room where the treasure was buried locked? When the wife of the Corregidor and the merchant of Xeres brought Charles Topcliffe [Ashley's clerk] to it, why was the door open and the treasure unburied? How was Charles alone able to prevent the Spaniard and his twelve armed men from taking the trunk away? What persons came to Charles between the time when he entered with the lady and the arrival of the Earl of Essex? Did the money bags seem full or empty? Why was the iron coffer, after taking two hours to break open, thrown into the well? Why was the money not weighed?[17]

From every side came assertion and counter-assertion. In mid-September a spy in the pay of Essex reported from Spain that the Spaniards considered the value of the plunder was between five and six million ducats, but 'the greatest part of the treasure of the cathedral church and town you missed, since it was hidden under the graves and vaults of the church'.[18]

At last Sir Antony's interrogators narrowed their inquiry down to one object, a gold chain. He admitted having acquired the chain in Cadiz, having taken it from the Corregidor,[19] without making any promise to restore it, 'which should be a thing in any man's judgement, especially such as know the wars and what it is to enter a town with the sword, as strange and rare as had been heard of'. The day before the inhabitants of Cadiz were sent to the mainland 'I saved and rescued the Corregidor, who was wearing the chain, from the fury and violence of many soldiers that set on him passing through the market place, having gotten him purposely grovelling on the ground and myself not able to prevail with my servants in the rescue, had not some of my Lord General's guards happily assisted'.[20] In spite of this answer the interrogators took the word of the Corregidor against Sir Antony, so eager were they to force answers out of him that might incriminate others. On 18 September Sir Antony wrote to Sir Robert Cecil: 'I most humbly entreat your good honour to procure my speedy delivery, or that I may be called and charged, hoping that it is not intended utterly to undo me, and to make me hateful and shameful by length of imprisonment to all the world.'[21]

At the end of the month, still in prison, he wrote again: 'Sir, I assure you this matter toucheth me to the quick, and savoureth so much of dishonour and ingratitude that had I my absolute liberty, (I cannot refrain to betray my weakness) I should either make bitter complaint to the Queen, or bring my action of champerty.'[22] In the end Sir Antony offered to hand over £530, the price he had received for the chain in Cheapside, and the Privy Council dropped the charge against him.

The accusation that the plunder of Cadiz demoralised and corrupted both fleet and army has been frequently made, but is unfair. Every soldier and sailor had known that, if the expedition failed, he would be lucky to receive from the Queen even that proportion of his pay not held back to cover the cost of his rations. Her meanness towards those who served against the Armada in 1588 was in everyone's memory.[23] Drake and his men had then made the *Nuestra Señora del Rosario* their prize, but no other seamen received any prize money. Similarly in 1596 those forced to give up plunder were likely to find themselves left in debt. Of course the crowds who welcomed them home saw nothing wrong in men disposing of plunder in whatever way seemed most profitable. The Queen had intended that the maximum damage should be done to the common enemy with the least cost to her Exchequer, and this they had achieved. Everything the government undertook was organised on the same semi-feudal basis. In peace and war pilotage, buoys and beacons were provided by the Lord High Admiral out of the proceeds of port dues. In the administration of justice no cause could succeed without fees and gifts. As Master of the Court of Wards Lord Burghley flourished on the income derived from managing the estates of the Queen's wards and arranging their marriages. Yet neither the Lord Admiral nor Burghley were corrupt in the sense that they acted against the public interest or abused their official powers. On the contrary, they and their contemporaries held that public and private interest could, and should, coincide.

Sir George Carew applied for, and obtained, soon after his return, a warrant to pay £423.0s.6d. 'to the cannoniers and other officers who attended about the ordnance' and to bestow £40 'as the Queen's bounty upon the poorer sort of cannoniers'.[24] Being long accustomed to administrative tasks of this sort, requiring accountancy accurate to the last penny, he found the insinuation that he had profiteered most offensive. His feelings were fully justified for, beside the registration of treasure, it had been his duty to see that all captured ordnance was handed over for the Queen's use. The manufacture and sale of guns and gunpowder was a valuable, and tightly controlled, royal monopoly. Merchant adventurers arming ships for private 'voyages of purchase' were anxious to avoid the expense and publicity attached to buying from the government. To slip a weapon or two out of the hands of the Master of Ordnance, and secrete them until all the malicious gossip had died down, was a great temptation. In a letter to Sir Robert Cecil, written from Cadiz, Sir George said that a hundred pieces of brass ordnance had been taken and he hoped soon to hear of more.[25] Although their value alone far outweighed the cost of the cannoniers' wages, the Privy Council went to extreme lengths to see that no other pieces were appropriated for private use. A letter sent to Carew Raleigh, Esquire, asked him to deliver to Sir George a piece of brass ordnance taken from a flyboat that had brought home fourteen brass pieces. Captain Henry Browne of Rye was required to surrender a brass falcon and three barrels of gunpowder.[26] The *Great Catherine* of Weymouth was reported to have brought back three pieces of brass ordnance, and the port authorities were ordered to insist on their surrender. The Privy Council also gave Sir George an open warrant to collect all ordnance that had been acquired by private persons or else its money value,[27] and sent separate letters to Sir Robert Southwell asking for two demi-culverins landed at Yarmouth; to Sir John Shelton and Captain Thomas Woodhouse for six pieces taken out of the *Ruby* of London; and to Captain Parker in Plymouth for two pieces landed out of the *Rainbow*. In view of all this Sir George wrote to Sir Robert Cecil:

'Since my arrival in Plymouth I understand that Her Majesty is informed of great sums of treasure gotten by me at Cadiz. It wounds me greatly that a suspect should be had that I would conceal anything from her by whose grace and favour I live, which when such dealing shall be proved against me, let me be exempted out of God's mercies. I will not now trouble your Honour with tedious apologies, but leave them until it shall please God to bring me to London to wait upon you at better leisure, at which time my innocency shall plainly appear unto you. My first care is to satisfy Her Majesty and my friends, not esteeming of the rest what they say or think. I will never crave a dishonest request of your Honour or desire to be protected in an evil course, but in matters honest and just I pray your aid to defend me from injurious reports. Your Honour hath been conceited of me that I would deal truly in all things, and this small absence hath not corrupted me. Then, by the Majesty of God I do protest, and by the religion of faith that ought to be between man and man, I neither had nor have in gold or silver coin, or in jewels, the worth of three ducats, but that which I have delivered, and in plate not above the value of twenty marks.[28] If to disprove my protestations good witnesses may be produced, I crave no favour; but because I know that no man can be found so audacious as to charge me upon his knowledge to give Her Majesty satisfaction, whose good opinion is more dearer to me than life, I am willingly ready to receive the Communion that they be true; which I would not do in a matter false to possess the King of Spain's treasure and crown.'[29]

## Chapter VI Notes

1. BM Otho IX 335.
2. W. C. Devereux, *Lives and Letters of the Devereux Earls of Essex*, London, 1853.
3. State Papers Domestic 1596.
4. Hatfield 44.18.
5. Duke of Northumberland's MS.
6. Hatfield 44.18.
7. State Papers Domestic 1596.
8. Hatfield 174.85.
9. Acts of the Privy Council Elizabeth XII.
10. Acts of the Privy Council Elizabeth XII.
11. Acts of the Privy Council Elizabeth XII.
12. Rummaging—to take the cargo out of a ship at anchor and carry it in small craft to the shore.
13. Acts of the Privy Council Elizabeth XII.
14. Hatfield 44.36, 44.37.
15. Hatfield 43.99
16. F. Bor, *Oorsprongh 1555–1600*, Amsterdam 1679/86.
17. Hatfield 44.65.
18. Hatfield 139.59.
19. It was the custom of Spanish noblemen to wear heavy gold chains about their necks. Many Spaniards leapt from the ships wrecked on the west coast of Ireland in 1588 and were drowned by the weight of the chains they wore. (Stephen Usherwood, *The Great Enterprise*, Bell and Hyman, London, 1982.)
20. Hatfield 44.90.
21. Hatfield 44.106.
22. Hatfield 43.24. Champerty was originally a feudal lord's right to a division of produce, but here a division of spoils is at issue.
23. State Papers Domestic 1588.
24. State Papers Domestic 1596.
25. Hatfield 42.23.
26. Acts of the Privy Council Elizabeth XII.
27. Acts of the Privy Council Elizabeth XII.
28. A marginal note states: 'Gold, silver, jewels and plate which I carried out of England is not comprised in this protestation.'
   Ducat: A coin of the Venetian Republic, circulating all over the world, worth about 9s (45p).
   Mark: A medieval coin worth two thirds of an English pound, i.e. 13s 4d (approximately 67p).
   Crown: An English silver coin worth 5s (25p).
29. Hatfield 43.66.

# VII

# Everyone
## taking his own course

No recriminations about plunder could obscure the overwhelming success of the 1596 expedition. The largest fleet and army to leave the shores of England up to that time had voyaged 1,500 miles of stormy ocean, captured and held a major port and returned safely with the minimum of loss. Attack as the best means of defence seemed to have been justified, and so, when news came that Philip II, so far from giving way to sickness and despair, was organising another armada, it was decided to strike in the spring of 1597 with a second Anglo-Dutch force. This was entrusted to the same commanders as before, with the exception of Lord Howard of Effingham, whom the Queen, with affectionate consideration for his age, kept at home. His exclusion was unfortunate, because Essex and Raleigh, having each enjoyed, and lost, Her Majesty's favour, were jealous of one another.

Soon after its departure the fleet was hit by a storm so severe that it was forced to return to port. Sir George was in command of the *St. Matthew*, the Spanish galleon taken at Cadiz and she, like the rest, had to be repaired. After this loss of time Essex decided to go for the Islands in order to intercept the treasure fleet from the Americas. This prize, though it lured him on in the same way that rumours of an *El Dorado* drew Raleigh to Venezuela, could not be achieved without exceptional luck.[1] Consequently the Islands voyage of 1597 was a fiasco. Raleigh reached Fayal days ahead, and before the main fleet arrived, plundered the island. Essex threatened to court-martial him. The other commanders intervened and it was decided to make a joint attack on San Miguel. During this operation the treasure fleet slipped into the impregnable port of Terceira. Essex, having achieved very little, brought the fleet home, and once more faced the Queen's anger. In a deliberate attempt to foster discord, she created the Lord High

Admiral, Howard of Effingham, Earl of Nottingham, and Essex, who did not conceal his disgust, indulged in shows of rage alternating with fits of melancholy, signs perhaps of incipient madness. When in 1599, a widespread rebellion broke out in Ireland, led by Hugh O'Neil, Earl of Tyrone, he and Sir George Carew were put in command of a large army and sent out with orders not to return till the rising had been crushed.

After a summer's indecisive campaigning, Essex met Tyrone alone and arranged a truce. Then, having handed over command to Sir George, he and a few companions crossed secretly to England and made with all speed for London. Finding the Queen had gone to Nonsuch House, near Richmond, the Earl immediately rode there and forced his way into the Queen's private apartments, where he begged her to accept the Irish truce. She, fearing some violence, first spoke soothingly, but before the day was over he was placed under arrest and taken to York House in the Strand, where he was kept isolated from his wife, family and friends until June 1600, and then formally charged with a long list of misdemeanours, found guilty, and banished to his country estates. Around the Queen Sir Robert Cecil and his adherents kept watch and guard. They knew that Essex was deeply in debt and could not hope to aspire to a courtier's life again unless she gave him some lucrative office. He, finding that she ignored his letters, began to plot a palace revolution. In February 1601 Essex, the Earl of Southampton, and their fellow malcontents, entered the City of London with drawn swords, hoping to raise a mob of supporters among those who had once cheered the homecoming from Cadiz, but they found none to join them. Armed guards from the Tower of London under the Constable, Lord Thomas Howard, trapped them in Essex House, Strand, and obtained their unconditional surrender. The Lord Chief Justice, sitting with seven other judges in Westminster Hall, conducted a brief trial. Raleigh was one of those who gave evidence against Essex, for he had been Captain of the Queen's guard at the time of the attempted coup. A jury of nine earls and sixteen barons pronounced Essex guilty of treason and he was beheaded.

Of the other leading rebels Essex's step-father, Sir Christopher Blount, and Sir Charles Danvers were beheaded, and Sir Gilly

Merrick hanged, drawn and quartered at Tyburn.[2] The Earl of Southampton was also condemned to death, but reprieved on the grounds of his youth and sent to the Tower. He had been a generous patron and friend of Shakespeare and news of these events worked like a fever in the poet's brain. Why had these proud, handsome young men allowed themselves to be corrupted by a jealous Queen and an immoral court? Not all their learning, wit and talent, not all their skill with sword and lance, had protected them from the consequences of inexperience, conceit and ungovernable temper. From these strands of bright gold and sable darkness he wove the stuff of his finest play, *Hamlet, Prince of Denmark*, and, when it was finished, wrote no more for two years.

Raleigh's fate, though slower in coming, was no less ruinous. Banished from the court when James I succeeded to the throne in 1603, and later accused of treason on the ground of alleged complicity in the plot to place Lady Arabella Stuart on the throne, he was condemned to death, but reprieved. After he had been twelve years in the Tower, the king released him for a voyage to Venezuela in search of gold. He came back empty-handed, having lost his elder son, killed in a skirmish with Spaniards. One condition for his release had been that there should be no hostilities with Spain, James having made peace in 1604. Raleigh was therefore arrested and, on the old charge of treason, condemned to death. Sir George Carew, now a peer, Baron Carew of Clopton, near Stratford-on-Avon, pleaded boldly for his cousin's life, but in vain. Raleigh, as he laid his head on the block, said to the executioner: 'So the heart be right, it is no great matter how the head lieth.' Lady Carew took special pains to comfort and care for Raleigh's widow and children.

Sir Francis Vere, after winning further victories over the Spaniards in the Netherlands, returned to the home of his ancestors in Essex and married a young wife. Their happiness was short-lived. He died in 1608 at the age of forty-nine, and was buried in Westminster Abbey in the presence of his brother and several others who had fought with him at Cadiz. His widow erected a tomb of white and black marble in his honour, modelled on that of Prince Engelbert of Nassau which he had seen in the Netherlands.

Lord Thomas Howard, created Baron Howard de Walden in 1597, received high honours from James I, who made him Earl of Suffolk and Lord Treasurer. The spoils of Cadiz were said to have contributed to the cost of the beautiful house he built at Audley End, the site of a former Benedictine monastery near Saffron Walden in Essex. His second wife, by whom he had seven sons and three daughters, was reputed to be very avaricious; in 1618 the Earl and Countess were prosecuted in Star Chamber for embezzlement, and kept in separate cells in the Tower of London for a short time. After paying a huge fine, £30,000, they were released. James I is said to have remarked on seeing Audley End: 'Too large for a king, but it might do for a Lord Treasurer.'[3]

Marriage presented Sir Robert Cross, who had commanded the *Swiftsure*, with a different problem. On 11 February 1607 he wrote to Sir Robert Cecil:

'Seeing there would be no employment for me after the decease of our late Sovereign Queen Elizabeth, I thought it my best course to betake me to a wife which then I did, thinking to have lived in peace with myself and the world, but now I hear say, that the poor fortune I had with her, the 2 parts thereof will be taken from me because she is a recusant. I have done my endeavour to alter her from it and have found that grace with the Lord Canterbury to come to my house and Sir Christopher Perkins twice, with Sir Edward Hoby and since Christmas a divine of the Lord of Canterbury, but [in spite of] all this neither I can yet alter her inward thoughts in that point.'[4]

Sir George, who remained in Ireland under a new commander, Lord Mountjoy, played a conspicuous part in the 'pacification' of the island. Both men returned in 1603, following the death of Elizabeth, and Sir George was appointed Vice-Chamberlain to James I's Queen, Anne of Denmark, and Receiver-General of all her revenues. From 1608 to 1617 he was Master of Ordnance for England (previously he had been Lieutenant), and also a member of the Council of the colony of Virginia. At court he was captivated by the wit and charm of young George Villiers, Marquis, later Duke, of Buckingham, who became a close friend of the King and of the heir to the throne, Charles. It was he who recommended that

Charles should after his coronation grant Carew the earldom of Totnes in Devon. Buckingham, who longed for military glory, led an expedition to Cadiz in 1625. Neither ships nor men were of the 1596 quality and, finding Cadiz completely refortified and strongly held, they suffered severe losses and accomplished nothing. Two years later the Duke undertook a still more hazardous adventure, the relief of the port of La Rochelle, where Huguenots were besieged by the army of the king against whom they had rebelled. He was again repulsed, but returned to Portsmouth determined to fit out another fleet. Here, in 1628, he was stabbed to death by a discontented officer, a murder that deeply shocked the King, who never found so close a friend again. The following year Totnes, who had reached the then considerable age of seventy-three, died in his rooms at the Savoy Palace. Thus in a short space Charles had lost two councillors on whom, as good friends of his parents, he had come to rely implicitly.

Lady Totnes conveyed her husband's body to Stratford-on-Avon for burial in Holy Trinity Church, very close to Shakespeare's grave. There, in the Clopton Chapel, she raised a tomb of marble and painted alabaster in his honour. This stands in a recess flanked by Corinthian pillars and adorned with glittering shields of arms. The recumbent effigies of the Earl and Countess lie on top of the sarcophagus, he in armour and both in the red robes denoting their rank. Below them are carved cannon balls, gun barrels, match cord and linstocks, reminders of his service as a Master of Ordnance. It lacks only one thing, a fitting English inscription. When his uncle Sir Peter died on active service in Ireland and was buried in Waterford Cathedral, the panegyric was delivered by the Lord Deputy, Sir Henry Sidney. His words could with equal justice commemorate Sir George:

'Here lieth now in his last rest a most worthy and noble gentle knight, whose faith to his prince was never yet stained, his truth to his country never spotted, and his valiantness in service never doubted—a better subject the prince never had.'

## Chapter VII Notes

1. The first Englishman to succeed in intercepting the galleons was Admiral Blake at Tenerife in 1656. Of him Charles II's minister Clarendon said: 'He was the first man that declined the old track . . . and despised those rules which had been long in practice to keep his ship and his men out of danger, which had been held in former times a point of great ability and circumspection; as if the principal art required in the captain of a ship had been to be sure to come safe home again.' *History of the Rebellion.*

2. Besides much other plunder, Sir Gilly Merrick brought home from Cadiz marble columns for his own tomb. When he was executed for his part in the Essex rebellion in 1601, his widow was refused custody of his dismembered body, and no tomb was erected to his memory.

3. The big house that remains today is less than half the original size.

4. Catholic Record Society, Miscellaneous Vol. 3. Because Sir Robert's wife was a Catholic recusant, that is, she refused to obey the law requiring all citizens to attend Church of England services, her estate became liable to two-thirds confiscation.

   The Lord of Canterbury, Archbishop Richard Bancroft, was the founder of Lambeth Palace Library, where the *Mary Rose* journal was discovered.

   Sir Christopher Perkins had once been a Jesuit, but renounced his vocation.

# Appendix I

Lambeth Codex 250, folios 344–362

## NOTE

The text of the *Mary Rose* Journall in Lambeth Palace Library is given below in the original spelling. It has not been practicable to print the lines in their original length, but Sir George Carew's amendments and corrections are indicated as follows:

Words in italics between square brackets were crossed out, e.g. 14 April [*towne*]

Words in Roman type between oblique strokes were inserted, e.g. 14 April /cytadell/

Words in Roman type between square brackets were written in the margin, e.g. 20 April [This day 24: sayle]

A Journall of all the particularities that fell out in the voyage under the chardge of the Lord Ad: Generals the Erle of Essex and the Lord Charles Howarde L: Hygghe Admyrall of England as allso of the names of all Commanders and great offycers with the Captaynes and volunterie gentlemen thatt appertayne to the Armye

A prayer made by the queene at
the departure of the fleet.

Moste omnipotent Maker and Garder of all our worldes masse, that
onely searchest and fadomeste the bottome of all our hartes
conceites, and in them seest the trewe originall of all our actions
intended; Thou that by thy forsight doest trewely discerne how no
mallice of revenge, nor quittance of iniurie, nor desyre of
bloodshede, nor greediness of lucre, hath bredd the resolution of
our now sett-out Armie, but a heedefull care, and warie watch that
no neglecte of foes, nor oversuertie of harme, might breede ether
daunger to us or glorie to them; These beinge groundes upon
which Thou didest inspyre the mynde, we humbly beseche with
bended knees, prosper the wourke, and with beste forewyndes
guyde the iourney, spede the tryumphe of their fame, and suertie
to the Realme, with the leaste losse of Englishe bloude.
To these devout petitions Lord geve thou thy blessed graunt.

f.344
A journall

11 On Easter day the 11th of April about 12: of the Clocke at nyght
the Erle of Essex tooke his leave of the queene att greenwyche,
the L: Admyrall beinge gone away from the courte before him to
bringe the shipps to Dover, the same nyght allso and the same
houre I took my leave of her Matie:

12 On Monday nyght the Erle of Essex came to Dover where he
founde the L: Adm: who was in Dover Roade havinge with him
the Raynebow, the Vantgard, the Tramontana the Trewlove,
the Crane, the Answere, the Lyons whellpe the Charles and the
Moone

13 On Tuedsday the 13th Aprill I came to Dover where I found the
Ad: generall honorablye accompanied with many noblemen and
gentlemen

14 On wenedsday the 14th there was nothinge done but as in the former dayes sendinge and retourninge messengers to the frenche k: who attended our Arryvall att Bollogne this day the [*towne*] /cytadell/ of Callis was wonne with a furious assault, the governour slayne and all the french put to the sworde but nott as then knowne unto us

15 On Thursday the 15th: the french kinges messenger before day came with lettrs from the kinge to the Erle of Essex, assuringe him thatt the [*towne*] citadell would hold out some few dayes longer and desyred him to hasten to meet him att St Ihon's Roade where he would attend his cominge, the same morning likewise the Ls: generalls received lettrs from her Matie gevinge them full authoritie and comyssion under the great seale to transporte forces over for the recovery of Callis, towardes the eveninge there came to Dover 3000 footmen devided into three regiments vyz: the Erle of Essex Reg: syr Thomas Wellfords Reg: and syr Coniers Clyffords Reg: wch were presentlye embarked, and the same eveninge the Ls: generalls the great officers comanding and Captens were all aborde ready to sett sayle, when att that instant a frenche gentleman from the Duke of Buyllon brought word of the losse of Callis whereuppon

f.344 verso

we retourned to Dover; this day allso the Arke, the Merhonor, the Lyon, the Mary Rose the Nonpareille and the Swyftsure came into Dover Roade, and allso Don Xtophero the kinge of Portingalls sonne, came out of france unto us:

16 On fryday the 16: earlye in the morninge the Duke of Buillon, Don Emanuel the kinge of Portugalls eldest sonne, and Don Antonio Perez with 12: persons or thereabouts landed att folkstone by Dover whom the Erle /of Essex/ with the Lordes and gentlemen brought into the towne, within one house, after his arryvall a fleet was dyscovered to the southward and the Alarme taken thatt it was the Spanysshe fleet, whereuppon in all possyble hast the Ls: generalls with the noblemen captens gentlemen and sonadians so gatt abord the shypps but in the end it proved to be netherlanders and then we retourned to Dover, the same day the Duke of Buillon, Don Emanuel and Antonio

126

Perez: Rode towards the Court: About supper tyme we had newse thatt syr francis Vere with his troupes were att an Anker before Bollogne

17 On saterday the 17 the 3: Regiments before mentioned were dysmissed and lettres was sent to syr Xtopher Blunt syr Ihon Wyngfield, and syr Rychard Wyngfield to pay these regiments and to dyssolve them: wch regiments were levied in Essex, Sussex, Surrey and Myddlesex, towards the eveninge syr francis Vere with his fleet came into Dover Roade, this day sundry merchants and Hoyes of our fleet came unto us from London:

18 On sunday the 18: the Erle of Essex in the Raynebow sett sayle for portsmouthe, and sr francis Vere for Plymouthe with his fleet, the L: Admyrall by a purswyvant was sent for by the queene to come to the court who Immediattlye posted thither, the Erle of Essex was lykewyse sent for but the messenger came short of his beinge under sayle before his cominge, about

### f.345

sonne settinge the wynde came from the south southe west and blew a stronge gale thatt we were enforced to wayghe Anker and fall to the downes

19 On Monday the 19:th we roade all the day in the Downes, the Erle of Essex havinge contrarye wynde landed att folkstone and from thence rode poast to the court

20:On Tuesdday the 20th: the Vantguard and the Raynebow sett sayle for plymouthe to wafte thither 600 sonadians Ostende that were shypped in flemyshe bottomes,

[MN (This day 24: sayle of Netherlanders thatt ayde us in this voyadge past by us towards plimmouthe:)]

dyvers /of the queens lesser shyppes/ and of our merchants shyppes went with them

Allso sundrye shyppes this day of our fleet left in the Thames came unto us whereof some of them stayed in the Downes with the Admyrall and some other made for plymouthe

21 On wenedsday the 21: towardes the eveninge the Nonpareille and the Lyons whellpe put over to the coast of france to gett intelligence of the enemies dessignes touchinge his purpose for Bollogne:

22:On Thursday the 22th: two shyppes of the North parts came to us to the downes, they were of coasters that were prest for this voyadge: all this nyght we had muche wynd:

23: On fryday the 23th: being st georges day we wayed /anker/ and fell downe in to dover rode:

24: On saterday the 24th: the wynde blew hard att southwest and south southwest wch enforced the fleet to wayghe Anker and fall into the Downes:

25 On sunday the 25th: the shyppes remayned in the Downes, and there taryed Monday the 26: day

27 On Tuedsday 27th: the shyppes came from the downes back into Dover roade

f.345 verso

28 On wenedsday the 28: in the morninge a fleet of flyboates passinge for spayne through the narrow seas were descryed by our shyppes, whereuppon they Immediatelye wayghed Anker and within three houres brought them into Dover /roade/ in all tenne sayles, about noone the L: Admyrall came to Dover.

29: On Thursday the 29th: in the forenoone the L: Admyrall went abord his shyppe, after dynner he dysmyssed two of the flyboates taken the day before, the other: 8: he put captens and men into them sufficyent to master the Dutches and so to attend his fleet, about two of the clocke lettrs came by a messendger of the chamber from syr Rob: Cecil to the L: Admyrall, to wyll hym in her Maties name to retourne to the Court wch once he purposed to have done but uppon bettre advice stayed, towardes nyght he caused proclamation to be made in Dover thatt all thatt were bound for this voyadge should uppon payne of deathe repayre to there shypps

30: After mydnyght on fryday morninge the 30: the L: Admyrall shott off a peece and wayghed Anker whom all the fleet presentlye followed holdinge our course westward: aboute noone athwart of pevensey bay we met with a fleet of Netherlanders in all 32: sayle with whom the Admyralle spake

f.346 [blank]

f.346 verso

On saterday the: 1: the wynd for the most part was att southeast and eastsoutheast the gale very slender and an exceedinge fayre day

On sunday the 2: a lyttle before /day/ the wynd began to blow hard att the Northeast and Hawsie, about seven of the clocke muche rayne att wch tyme we entered into the sound of Plymouthe where we came to an anker:

about: 2: of the clocke afternoone there was one in the Mary Rose duckt at the Mayne yardes Arme:

At our landinge we found the Erle of Essex in Plymouthe and all the great officers and captens of the Land Army where we attended the Cominge of the Rereadmyrall with the Remaynder of the fleet, and in the mean tyme spent the dayes in trayninge and sortinge the Companies into Regiments

On fryday [*morninge*] /the 21:/ about 7: of the Clock /in the morninge/ the Rereadmyrall came to an Anker in the sound of Plymouthe with the resydue of the fleet after whose arryvall the tyme was industriously spent in revytaylinge the fleet and supplyinge of all other defects in so muche as uppon the last /of May/ all the Land Companies and the whole Army were shypped and the greatest part of the shyppes thatt were in Cattwater warped out into the sound

f.347

June 1.On [*monday*] /Tewsdaye/ the first about fowre a clock in the morning the Admirall Howard shott of /a/ warning pece to give knowledg to the fleete of his departure and aboute 7 of the clocke the wynd being at west north west set sale and putt forth to the sea after whome did follow a good part of the fleete confusedly, and at 12: a clocke the Vice-admirall sett sale. towards /night/ the Admirall Essex the [*flemish*] Admirall of Holland, and the Reare Admirall wyth all the rest of the fleete putt to the sea. all wch day and night following the wynd holding shyft at west north west we plyed of and on between the Ram head and foy

2 On wednisday morning we found our selves a thwart of foy not above 3. leagues from the shore the wind as before. all wch day we plyed up and downe tyll towardes fowre a clock att which /tyme/ finding the wynd [*south*] south west, the Admyrall Howard came roome for the sound of Plymouth after whome the

fleete followed and before eight a clocke weare all att anker part in the sound and part att /Cawshant/ [deletion] baye. /and/ mediatly [*after*] the Generalls [*came to anker they*] gave commandment upon payne of death that no man should go a shore which don, the selected cownsell /together with the Admirall, Vice: and Rearead: of Holland/ mett aboard the Admirall Howard To resolve what enterpryse was fyttest to be undertaken for the annoyance of the Spanish king. wheare it was concluded by generall opinion of the cownsell and with the assent of the Lords generalls that Cales in south Spayne was fyttest to be attempted as a place of importance to impech the enimy most easy to surprysed and in it self rich, besides the good [*assurance*] posibilytie to sack Porta Reall Porta Sta Maria St Lucar, and Sherez, as also to burne and take suche shipps and gallies /as/ [*and*] should be found in the places aforesaide. it was also resolved that no part of Spayne should in any /case/ be aproched or attempted by any of our fleete nor if we could otherwayes chuse come wythin sight of the spanish coast untyll we came to the height of Cape St Vincent comonly cawled the southwardly cape. and further if it should so happen that by fowle wether our fleete should be severed it was there lyke wyse decreed that /all the/ [*such*] shipes [*as*] should make there rendezvous at cape St Vincent and those that should fortune first to make the Cape should ly of, not wythin sight of the land untyll som one of the Admiralls of the Squadrones weare come up from whome they were to resave directyon and to attend that sayd Admirall tyll the hole fleete weare united, /And/ that every /sea/ Captayne might have notice hereof it was lykewyse thought good that /the/ said captaynes should generally have a byllett sealed up with the Lordes generalls seales wherein should be sett downe these resolved directyons [*which lyketh uppon*] wyth commandment upon payne of death not to breake open the same untyll they should be by such extremitie inforced thereto.

### f.347 verso

The next nine lines, describing the final departure on 3rd June, are lightly crossed out and transcribed on the lower part of the page. They appear on page 131.

130

which sayd directions weare sett downe in these wordes, and dispersed at sea with all possible expedition

Whereas it may happen (as offen is experienced) that some of the fleete may by fowle wether or otherwayes loose the companie of his squadron of the fleete, for the better prevention of the great inconveniences usually thereby folowing, we do hereby straightly wyll and comand all Captaines and maysters of everie such ship as shall by any occasion so lose companie, that they faile not to shape and direct /their/ course to the height of the Cape St Vincent otherwayes called the South cape in Spain making onely the land thereof, and not to come so neare as to be discovered from it by the enymy, wheare a cople of Pinases or some other meete vessels shall porposely attend for their further direction. And if they shall not find any vessell their to this porpose, then shall they make of and on their in the height of that Cape tyll some Admirall of a squadron shall come whose direction they shall obey for there further repayre, whereof you may not fayle at your uttermost perills

Abord the dew Repulse in Cawshant Bay the second of June 1596

Essex:     C Howard

Poster:

    howbeit o/r/ mening is if you find us not at the Cape that you come imediatly for Cales in Andulazia

The direction of the back side the byllett sealed up—as foloweth—and delyvered to everie ship in hec verba

If you be seperated from the fleete by fowle whether or otherwayes you shall herein fynd to what place you shall repayre, tyll when you shall not open the inclosed upon payne of deathe

3. On Thursday morning the Lord Admirall Howard went in his Barge to Plymouth to pres forth the [blank] in place of the Jonas wherein mr.fyshborne was captaine and Captaine Collyers companie transported: for that the day before whilst we weare at sea the ship being old, leakes did grow so fast uppon her as with greate travaile she was kept from sinking: and aboute ten of the clock the Lord Admirall Howard wyth his squadron following him set sale to sea againe, the wynd being at North west: and after him the other Admiralls wyth there squadrons followed, so

as the Reare Admirall wyth the last of the fleete weare by fowre a clock under sale.

4. On fryday and Saterday the wind continewed for the most part
5. at [sow] west north west, and north west, with some calmes.

### f.348

6. On sonday morninge about an hower and hallfe before day, the weather beinge fowle, and a port gale of wynde att the Northwest, the Mary Rose spent her mayne yard, whereuppon (to geve warninge of thatt myschance to the fleet) she shott of: 2: peeces and in the shrowdes /did/ hange out tow lyghts a mans heyght one above another, att wch sygnes the Rereadmyrall with many other shyppes Came Roome unto her, to understand whatt dystresse she was in and to geve her hellpe, but thankes be to god the breakynge of the mayne yard was all the hurt she receved /after in few dayes repayred/ all this day the wynd contynewed still (but dry) att the Northwest, with a styffe gale and a growne sea, about noone we found our sellves in 48: degrees and odd mynutes:
7. monday and tewsday fayre wether [and we continued our course]
8. the wynd being as before
9. wednisday [night] all the fore parte of the day [almost a] /calm/ towardes the evening [the wynd blowing styff] /stormy with a styffe gale/ at the north west and [wyth some rayne] wherewith the Swyftsure spent her fore mast, whereupon the Lordes Generalls wyth the hole fleete tacked aboute and made in wyth her, but thankes be to god, there was no man hurt, and the next day the mast [made serviceable] fyshed
10. Thursday thre of our fleete being far a hede us /and to the/ leward [being] sopposed to be strangers had chase given them by order from the generalls: the same day a smal man of france that came from the coast of Spayne came into the fleete and went aborde the Admyrall Howard wyth some reportes of those partes, butt not of consequence.
11. fryday /in the morning/ the Lord Admirall Howard went abord the Lord Generall Essex upon whose coming the Queenes Armes a flag appointed /to be a token/ to call together the selected

cownsell was hung on the misne shrowdes, at sight whereof the cownsell aforesayd repayred to the shyppe, at which consultation the Admirall: Vicead and Rearead: of Holland weare present, [*at wch tyme*] /where/ it was projected [*and concluded untyll uppon the sight*] in what manner the squadrons wyth there Admiralls should make there aproche to the Bay of Cales, what places fytt to land the companyes, and in what manner to attempt /the towne/ and such shyppes and gallyes as should be fownd in the Roade. butt yett not so concluded, butt left to such further consideration as should be thought necessarye upon vew of the place. After dynner a flag of St Georg [*was putt*] (a token [*to*] assigned to call a comon cownsell of Captaynes and mrs. was hanged in the shrowdes as before, uppon whose repayre these questions weare propownded, first what height we weare in which for the most part was taken to be next to 42. degrees to the southward, secondly, [*what leages*]

### f.348 verso

how many leagues they sopposed the fleete at /that/ Instant to be west from the shore. there opinions were sondry [*and*] /but/ the greatest part of the maysters sopposed aboute 30: leages. thirdly what course weare best to be sald for the dobling of Cape St Vincent wch after long debating [*it*] our course was resolved to hold sowth and by east whereof all the captains and maysters weare wylled to take knowledg: with comandment to attend diligently upon the Admiralls of there particoler squadrones. And further thatt: the Regimentes might not be unprovided of munitions direction was given by the Lordes Generalls unto the mr. of the Ordinawnce to delyver unto every Coronell a convenient proportion. After all which the Cownsell [*and*] Captaynes /and maysters/ parted. This day also a comission was delivered under the Lordes Generalls handes and directed to S/r/ Georg Carew mr. of the Ordinance to Antony Ashely secretarie for the cownsell of war, and Marmaduke Dorrell Vittalor Generall for this Army. to this tenure insewing.

[MN   Also this day aboute 3: of the clocke in the after noone: thre fly-boates tow of Amsterdame and one of mydelbrough weare taken after some resistance made to the Trewlove whereof mr. Rychard Lewson was Cap: who did first hayle them and by the ayde of the Lyones [*Sr. Christopher Blun*] wherein Sr. Christopher Blunt was transported [*and by the Roe Buck, who*] These flyboates came dyrectly from Cales loaded wyth salt, wynes etc: and home ward bound; and in them was fownd in Barells silver [blank] and in bags, of gold: [blank] there was kylled of the flemings in the Admirall who made gretest resistance; 3: men, whereof the mr. was one and sondry hurte; and gave some intelligences of the state of Cales. where there is no preparation extra: ordinarie for there defence for that as they reported they weare there perswaded that our land and sea forces weare to be imployed for defence at home and that when they came from thence there was 13: sale of Spanish shyps and one greate dane outward bownd deeply laden for the Indies [*for whose defence*] 10: of the kings shipes of warr the St Phylippo being Admirall weare in a redines at St Lucar to fall into the Bay of Cales. to accompany these mrchants, for there guard to the Indies]

### f.349

12. Saterday the weather fayre and the wynd very handye att noone we found our selves in 40 degrees and 50 mynutes:

13 sunday in the morninge about six of the clocke uppon our larbord syde the Brelings appeared wch was the first land we made from our departure from plymouthe towards night a Carvell was taken and brought into our fleete being a fisher man of [*Panace*] Peniche, also the same athwart the Rock the John and francis wherein mr. Dorrell the Vittaler was Cap: took a flyboote called the fawcon of flushing loaden with Oyles, and Wyne in her was also silver [blank] of gold; [blank] she was loaden in Maiorsia with Spanish goodes and bownd as we soppose for lisbona; this shyp; the Swann wherein mr. Rychard westen was Capt. /the night before/ [*was by hym*] layd /this shyp/ a board in whych feight the mr. of the flyboote was slayne and eight men hurte: and in mr. westens shyp[2] /1/ slayne and [*13*] /11/ hurte butt in the end the Swan brake her /beake heade and/ boltesprytt and fell of, butt er the pryse could recover Lysbona whether they sayd they intended to go to burry there mr. and to

repayre there harmes /she/ was after layd abord and taken [by] as aforesayd by mr. Dorrell

14. Monday the fleebote taken by mr.Dorrell the day before came into the fleete: and aborde my L. Generall Essex the selected cownsell dyd volentaryly meete: where /consultation was had, in what manner/ [*it was resolved that Sr walter*] the towne should be attempted, and the shyps secured

[a pen has been lightly drawn through the following nine lines] Rawligh wyth all his Squadron should enter into the Bay of Cales as far as Puntall; as well to surpryse the marchantes shyps outward bownd for the Indies as to land the regimentes of the Earle of Sussex and S Rychard wynfildes at that istmos not far from Puntall wheare the land is narowest it was lykewyse agreed that the lord Thomas Howard on the south syde of the foresayd Istmos should land the tow regiments of Sr. Christopher Blunt and Sr Thomas Gerrard: whych 4 Regiments are to be comended by such persons, and to follow

### f.349 verso

[*as the Lord Generalls shall then appointe the cawse of whose implyment on that part is to forbyd any forces /from the land/ to reskew the Towne of Cales at that syde. The Lord Generalls them selves not yett resolved what course to take in there owne persons but according as occasion should be mynistered. betwene St Sebastian and the block house of Los Puercos, in the bay of Catelina it was resolved the Lord Generall E*] Also this day there was towe Carvayles taken and the land of Montfigo was discovered.

15. Tewsday morning we dobled the Cape St Vincent: and that day the Ro buck brought in a Carvayle, to whome she had over night given chase, butt the men to save them selves ran agrouwnd and abandoned the vessell

That day the Lordes and Cownsell dyned abord the Vice-Admirall the Lord Thomas Howard. wheare consideration was had and direction under the Lord Generalls handes given to /the/ [*every*] Admiralls of Squadrons, etc coronells of Regimentes in what order and forme the Army should be landed as foloweth.

Abord her M/ts/ shypp the Merehonor the 15 of June reqd.

ordered and resolved by the Generalls in Cownsell for the landing at Cales.

Thatt the Admirall of every Squadron have all his boates belonging to his squadron in a redines to land these men that are now in the shypes of his squadron

Thatt if he have tow regimentes to be landed by his sayd boates he shall of those regimentes land equall numbers, for the first, second, or as mani tymes as the boates come to fetch the men

Thatt everie Colonell beinge one of those that shall have the point at the landing shall land a third part of his regiment wch third part shalbe of his best men and those to come wythout any ensigne wyth them becawse no ensigne shalbe engaged tyll the place of descent shall be secured

Thatt the said regimente shall observe the same order in the attempting the towne or forces except other direction be given by the generalls Viz that ensignes be kept where the gretest body and strength of the troopes is tyll the other third part have tryed the possibylitie of the attempt

That the boates that shall land the troopes shall all be marshalled in Ranke according to such a front as the place of descent wyll permytt wch order of mrch in Rowing or saling they shall presisely keepe, no boate thrusting out of a hynder ranke into a former, nor shrynking out of the former into a hynder, of wch order such land men as command the troopes and such sea men as direct the boates shall give a stryct accompt.

### f.350

Thatt all the boates in the hynder rankes shall have there ey on the boate thatt leadeth them, and all the boates in the first ranke shall observe the boate thatt is appointed to be their guyde and director wch boate shall carry eyther a st Georges flag or a whyte Pendent in the Prow and shall keepe in the heade of the first ranke at the going of from the shypes

Thatt when the Drom that beateth the first ranke shall beate a march they shall all row forward such a pace as the first leadeth who shall be appointed to row no faster than the slowest boate may conveniently keepe companie and if the leading boates stay and the Dromes cease beating then shall they all stay, or if the sayd leading boate lead backward, or torne her course som other way he shall do the lyke

The first boates being landed shalbe led to a fytt place to make a stand to secure the grownd of descent, tyll the ensignes and the gros be landed

Thatt when the Admirall at the landing place shall receave his white pendant and sett it above his flag on the mayne top then shall the soldyers putt them selves into boates to be landed as it shalbe sett downe:

16 Weddnisday in the morning a Caravell was discovered unto whome the Lord Thomas Howard and serten shypes of his Squadron gave chase, and being taken there was found none but /12:/ Inglish men in her: Saylers aperteining to Mr Bromelyes shyp of London, wch was then in Barbary to take in her marchandyze during wch tyme, these maryners bought this carvayle, to gett purchase, on the coast of Algarbe. by them we understood that we weare not discovered from the Mayne

17.Thursday as since the thirteneth of this month the wynd held fair at east, and calmy, in so much as in all these dayes we could not gett to the eastward of Cape St Maries

### f.350 verso

18.fryday in the morning very early from out of the Arke a strandg shyp was discovered to be in our fleete, who in the night unadvisely fell into the same, and did her best to acquytt her self out of it, butt after tow shott made unto her from the Admirall, she came abord him, she was a shyp of waterford, thatt the day before came from Cales she did assure us, thatt we weare not discovered on the coast, and that in Cales they lyved in great securyte not having any knowledg of our being at sea. by her also we understood that there was sixtie in /the roade before/ Cales

137

outward bownd for the west Indies above 20: sales of marchantes and six Gallyons of the kinges, whereof the St. Phylyppo was Admirall to waft them in ther voiadge. and further eyther 14: or 16: Gallyes in St Mary Porte and Cales whereof dyvers of them were not yett in a redines for the sea. [and from] also [they] /she/ gave us knowledg of 2: Argosies bownd for Lysbona that putt to the sea imediatly after her. The same morning the Lord Generalls in Cownsell, mett abord the Arke, wheare order was given thatt the warspyte, the Mary Rose, the Quyttance the Lyones the Trewlove, and [the] dyvers others to the /number of 17: sale/ should tacke aboute to the coast to mete wyth the Argosies aforesayde. And also, in Cownsell it was resolved that the Lord Generall Essex should land as it should please him to direct, the land forces for the attempting of the towne of Cales, and the Lord Admirall Howard wyth the best of the shypes of war should, att his direction eyther give uppon /the/ shypes there in the roade or /to/ garde them from escape untill the towne weare surprysed, and lykewyse /Cap:/ Alexander Clyfford

#### f.351

wyth the Raynbow, the Vantgard, the Alcedo, the Affection and thre Hoyes should come to anker before St Mary Porte, to assure the Gallyes there from doing annoyance to our fleete, further this daye towardes evening: the Lord Admyrall Howard wyth serteyn shypes gave chase to

[blank]

19. Saterdaye the fleete wch was appointed to attend Sir walter Raligh holding there course inward to the shore, about 9: a clock in the morning discovered to the eastward between 9: &: 14: sale, whereof one of them was a[n exceeding] great Gallion who bare wyth our forefoote untill she came wythin a leage of us and then plyed up for the wether, Immediatly after, a mighty fog about 4: a clock fell so thyck as it was not possible for one shyp to discry an other a cable lenth of, in this fog Sir Georg Carew, and Captain Gifford who had beene abord the Reare Admyrall /in his shyps boate/ wyth much ado came abord a small Pinies and by a

138

clock at night by great hap lyghted on the Quyttance, Capten Gyffords shyp. where looking out for

f.351 verso

there Admiralls light they espied one to the wynd ward, wch they followed, and before breake of day ran so far that course, as they weare at 5: fadoms water [*to the*] close abord the shore to the east of Clixiona, in this course, one of the spanish fleete next sale to the Acquyttance came agrownd sopposed by the acquyttance to be sr. walter Ralighs Hoy: wherefore direction was given to a Carvaile, formerly taken by our fleete to repayre to the shyp agrownd, And to bring away her men, and to burn her; butt she findinge the same to be a Spanyard bare Rome, the Admirall and fyve others, whose light the Acquyttance had followed all night, by the breake of day came wythin muskett shott of her, and made to the shyp agrownd, not daring to approche her for feare of the gross fleete, wch. weare a leage to the wether of her: when they [*discovered her*] came to the wrack they gave her no ayde butt bore on ther course to the west:

f.352

[20 *Sonday morninge about 6: a clock the hole fleete came to Anker in the Roade betwene St Sebastians, at the town of Cales. from whence they discovered wythin the Bay: the fleete of shypes and Gallies, as the Irish mr. chant had before reported: not long after, the wind blew a styff gale at west and west and by south, wch made a greate byllow in the Road, yet notwythstanding, though to no porpose we attempted the landing of companies [deletion] wch we found impossible, whereupon, the Generalls shott of warning peces and weighed, tacking about on the steerboard and came to Anker anew right afore cales wythin shott of fowre shypes, a fleete, whereof the Lord Generall Essex and Sir Georg Carew weare the first and untyll night there passed many greate shott from those five shypes and the enymy*]

20. Sonday morning about 6 a clock we came to Anker wyth the hole fleete before Cales over against the Callette or midraught & by the Castell of St Sebastians, wheare we proposed to make our

139

discent, butt the Lordes generalls having consideration of the danger we should enter into in landing our companies by reason of the greatenes of the Byllow altered there porposes, and in this storme, the Raynbowes boote with 15 men was overtorned, towards the evening the Lord Generall Essex weighed his Anker, and fell into the bay after whome the hole fleete folowed, where at that present directly before the towne, nothing was done more than the delyvery of certain shott from the Spanish fleete and the towne uppon the Repulse the Mary Rose and the Alcedo whych shypes ryd nearest unto them and answered them wyth the lyke salutations.

21 Monday in the morning after sonne rysing the Lordes Generalls and cownsell mett abord the Arke wheare it was resolved thatt the L. Thomas Howard Viceadmirall of the fleete in the Nonparylle sr walter Raleigh Reradmyrall in warspyte, the Lord Martiall in the Raynbow, the mr. of the Ordinance in the Mary Rose, Sr. John wingfild in the Vangard

f.352 verso

Sr. Robert Southwell in the Lyon, Alexander Clyfford in the Dreadnought and Captayn Cross in the Swyftsure, wyth sertein merchantes and Dutch men of warr should feight wyth the fleete, the Lordes Generalls wyth the rest of the fleete to be under sale, butt not to come in danger or to feight, onles the shypes resyted weare distressed whyle this was in cownsell determining the spanish fleete weighed and came under sale falling further into the bay towardes Port Reall: the marchantes shyppes ronning up the Ryver as far as they could, and the king's shypes wyth others stayd at Anker over agaynt Puntall garded wyth all the Gallyes except tow left [at] close by Cales Sr walter Raleigh having weighed sooner than the rest, made after them leading our fleete in wyth greate bravery and in passing by the towne, infynyte store of shott was spent betwene, our shypes, the town and gallyes, much to their damadg and nothing to our los, when we weare come wythin a resonable distance of the enimy whear they weare at Anker, we lykewyse ankered, and roade as conveniently as the strayghtnes of the channell would permytt and imedyatly a

140

furyous battery on eyther syde was intertayned. The shypes of
ours on whome the substance of the feight dyd consyst weare ten
sale the next to the Admyrall of Spayne was Sr. walter Raleigh to
second hym not long after the Battery begon, my L. Generall
Essex contrary to the former resolution contynewed in hys
course and came in hys owne shyp to anker close by Sr. walter
Raleigh, chandging shott for shott abondently, then the lord
marshall, then Sr Georg Carew, after hym my Lord Thomas
Howard in the Nonperylly, then Sr Robert Southwell, Captain
clyfford Captain Cross and the Alcedo. And after the feight had
contynewed a good whyle, my lord Admirall understanding
thatt the Earle of Essex was gon in

f.353

being unable to come in with his owne shype pestered up wyth
the gross of the fleete a far of, went abord the Myrrohonor who
by that tyme was in feight. Aboute six a clocke in the morning
the feight in our passadge by the towne and gallyes dyd begin,
aboute 9 the gallyes rowed to the great shypes to gyve them ayde,
but wythin one our after the gallyes shronke for there gard and
fell under Puntall whych fort dyd beate us a far of wyth their
ordinance aboute one a clock in the after noone the enimy
weighed to wythdraw them selves further into the Ryver,
whereuppon the Generalls resolved to board them, butt so many
in there shypes weare slayne, and every man so much dismayd,
as neyther dyd soldyer attend to his pece nor maryner hys
service, whereby there shypes ronn a grownd, and before we
could come to them there men leaping into the water, weare
drowned in greate numbers and those that escaped Ran to Port
Reall The substance of the enymys fleete was 4: of the kings
Armados: to say: the St Phylyppo Admyrall: the St Matheo
Viceadmirall. the St Andrea, and the St Tomaso, towe great
gallyons wch came from Lysbon 3: greate freighgates of the
kinges, the Admyrall vicead: and Rearead: of Nova Hispania,
wch last admyrall was the greatest shyp in all the fleete thre
Raguzcans in all shypes of warr 21 and of marchantes aboute 40.
sale more, besydes 19 gallyes of the best in spayne: /namely the/
and all

141

[Capitana the Admirall in whom was Don Juan de Puertocarrero Leutenante to the Adalantado and brother to the Conde de Palma Occasion [*Admi*] in whome was cap: the marques de St Croce: Cap: Xpofer de Sanches Padiglia: capt: /Juan de Osorio/ [*Conde de Ribadania*] de Bracamonte Patrona: cap: Don Diego de Mendoza nephew to the duke of Infantasgo fama: cap: Julian Hortado Eugenia D: Gonsalvo [*Patrona*] Luna. Cap: Medina Manrrique. D: Garsia St.Barbara. Cap: Alcate Lucera. Cap: Colero espagnola Leona. Ernando de Sarita Bassan. D: Anto: de Jubilatar fortezza [*vigilansa*] Esperanza. Diego Ordomaez Temeraria. Cap: Sepeda Lieva. Pedro Vargas Serena. Cap. Badillo St Yago Juan de Arango 19

The los that we resaved [*this*] in this sea service was one flyboote unfortunately fired by negligence of /by some of/ the same shype: and not 30: slayne [*in the*] /by the/ enimy: and of them butt one gentyllman, sonne to Customer smyth: [*moreover*] /besides one/ other pinnas of Sr. Robert Sothwell, whych in layinge the great shyppe abord, whylest she was burning was fired by her, the men all saved.]

there shypes weare laden rychly and bownd for the Indies amongst these thatt came agrownd the St Phylyppo and the St Tomaso sett them selves presently on fyer, to our exeding glory and joy thereby assured of the victorye, the St Mattew and St Andrew weare left on grownd abandoned by them and taken by us. This Don the Lord Generall Essex dyd instantly shyp into long boates and Pinnaces aboute 3000 of hys land companyes of every regiment a part, accompaned wyth most of the officers and gentylmen thatt weare for land service

f.353 verso

[MN St Philippo Cap: Diego de Soto St Mathew. D. Juan de Arsega St Andrew St Thomas La Capitana D: Diego Alfonso flores Captain generall of the Indian fleete.]

landing them in a lyttle bay betwene Puntall, and Cales and from thence mrched dyrectly to the south syde of the Iland, the enymy from the towne beholding our troopes sallyed forth bothe horse and foote to impede our approch unto it, the L. generall thinking by there contenance that they porposed to feight advanced part of hys forces towardes them for Sr Conyers Clyfford Sr Chrystopher Blunt and Sr Thomas Gerrard wyth their regimentes weare sent to assure the strayght of the land whych was not far from us. Sir John Wingfyld. leading in the vandgard was charged by the enymys horse, who stoode them bravely and wyth his pyke wonded Don Nunno de Vylla Vincenza, one of the chiefest cavallyers, the enymy fynding our stand so fyrme retrayted in Route to the port of the Towne pressing to gett in to the same in such hast as they left many of there horses behynd them The Lord Generall being evermore wyth the foremost having now wonne the dytch in gayning whereof some men were lost, and Sir Jhon wingfyld and Captayne merkyrk [*slayne*] shott, ascended the Rampire and cawsed hys owne collors to be first advanced uppon the wall, at sight whereof the enymy fled and dyvers of our men some over the wall some at the corner of the wall entered who opened the port for the generall, in every streete resistance was made wyth los on eyther syde even unto the mrkett place where in lyke manner from the toppes of the houses and wyndowes they shott many of our men, and amongst the rest (long after we weare possessed of that place) Sir John wyngfyld was slayne, the Lord Marshall in the meane tyme wyth some soldyers led towardes the Pryory, whereunto dyvers

f.354

[The names of certein of the best sort that weare in Cales when our fleete came before it Maximiliano de Austria Bishop elect of Cales, before Abat of Alcala la Real in the kingdome of Granada: went to Cyvill.

Don Antonio Sapeta old bishop of Cales elect bishop of Pampelona in Navarra: in Cyvill

Don Antonio de Raya: bishop of Cusco in the kingdom of Peru, delyvered freely.

143

Ernando de Guemes a Biscanin, Cap: of the Castell of Cales, delivered.

Martien de Rigoien, a Biscain Cap: of the fort St. Phiyppo, delivered.

Don Roderigo de Villa Vincentia Dean of Cales, imploied to Cyvill wyth his brother to procure the ransom of the rest but never retorned.

The Prisoners names: D. Antonio Giron de Cuniga of the kingdome of Toledo Corrigiador of Cales, Don Paio Patino Archdecon of Cales, Pedro Guttieres flores de Conseino de las Indias, president de la casa de la Contrastation de Indias de Criula Pedro de Castylla Juas de las Indias in Cadiz]

### f.354

men of good qualytie weare fled for succor who uppon honour rendered them selves that night, a strong gard was held for as yett the old towne uperend wherein the Castell is seated [*and whereunto*] and whereunto in a manner all the peple of the towne had putt them selves: Towardes sonn setting the L: Admyrall the Lord Thomas Howard Sir Walter Raleigh and others whome we left abord came to us: The castell at Puntall imdeatly after our landing was by the gard abandoned and entred not by the Hollanders. Captain Samuell Bagnall in this service deserved much honor for he came often to the push of the Pyke and was wonded in sondry places, in reward whereof that night the lord generall made hym Knight, in wynninge of thys towne above 200 men. Sr Edward Wyngfyld Sr Charles Percy Captain Harvy, captain Hambridg & others weare hurte.

22 Tewsday morning those at the towne that had taken the castle for there safetye hung forth a flag of trewce and [*and des*] requested a tretye wch granted [*craved pardon be granted*] the Corigiador and fyve others of the best amongst them came to the generalls, and concluded wyth them fyrst to yeld to there mercy, offeringe for further composytion to pay in regard of their lyves 120 /ñ/ ducates: and to putt into

there handes fyftye of the best amonst them for pledges tyll the ransom should be payd wch being accepted the generalls of there favor provided shypping to imbark the women and religious persons to pas to port St Mary and the meaner sort had convoy by land towards the brydg. This contract was interchangeably subscribed, and to assure the retorne of these messingers to the Castell from the violence of the soldyers the mr. of the ordinance was cõmanded to conveigh there and to se the keyes of the castle delyvered to Captayne Savadge to whome at thatt instant my lord gave the honor of knighthood /The rest of this day tyll late night was spent in putting forth of the castle the meaner sorte and warning the reste/. That done the Captaine of the [*castell*] /fort/ of St Phylyppo rendered the same and hym self to the generalls mercy: Also this daye Sir Conyers Clyfford, Sr Chrystopher Blunt, and Sir Thomas Gerrard wyth there regiments came into the towne

f.354 verso

who the daye before had bene sent to secure that straight of the land against such enymyes as should be sent from the mayne to assayle us in the reare gard of our march to the towne, who as it should seeme mistaking his directyon mrched on 12: myle to the brydge called Puente de Suaco, and in this [*march*] Jorney they weare greatly annoyed by a castle held by the Spaynardes neare to the brydg, by a barrycado upon the /brydg/ for end of the brydg and by the gallyes drawne downe to thatt place wyth porpose to pas thorough, all this not wythstanding they lodged there thatt night, destroyed some part of the brydg, and threw into the ryver tow peces of artilyrie that they found there. In the morning they retrayted whome the enymy followed afar of cutting the throats of such our disordered soldyers as by dronknes had dissabled them selves eyther to march or move. so as it is thought we lost aboute 200 men, most thereof rather by there owne default /& dronknes/ then by the enymyes sword. after the departure of our troupes the kings gallyes passed through the brydg and gott a seabord the Iland and rowed to Rotta.

23 weddnesday the [*rest*] gros of the Spanish fleete, thatt escaped

from us by running up towardes Porta Reall, by the com̃and-
ment of the Duke of Midena weare sett on fyer in so much
as of shypes of war and merchantes there was taken and burnt
by us and them aboute 57. sale, the richest fleete that ever
was bownd for the Indyes beinge valewed by estimation 12
mylyons

24. Thursday all the prysoners the pledges excepted, and such as
weare not comprysed in the contract weare delyvered under safe
convoy: In the afternoon a cownsell was held at [my] /the/ lord
generalls lodging wheare it was disputed whether it was fytt to
keepe this cyttye or nt. and concluded by generall opinion uppon
good reasons there alledged, that it was fytt to be held, and to
thatt porpose to dispatch a mesinger to her mtie [*in this tyme of
consultation*] /and in lyke manner Sir Edward Hobly./ to be sent
[*into*] /forthwyth into/ Barbery to the king of morocco, as the
generalls [*dyd*] formerly had determyned.

### f.355

In this tyme of consultation, thre captaynes of the gallyes wyth
letters from Don Juan de Puertocarrero Leutenant generall for
the Adelantado of Castyllia to the Lordes generalls, the
contentes whereof weare to intreate the delyvery of prysoners
eyther for ransom or exchandg in answer whereof the Lordes
dispatched captayne Robert Cross, Captain watson and Captain
Mydelton wyth their letters signyfying that already they had
ransomed so many as they porposed: the ladyse [*gentylmen*] and
meaner peple of eyther [*sedes*] sexes wch weare thowsandes in
number they had frely released, if he would send them the
Inglish prysoners in the gallyes and else wheare they would take
it in good part

25. fryday captayn Cross wyth the rest retorned the answer was
that the Spanyardes dyd promyse to dispatch answere after
hym

26. Saterday aboute 3 a clock in the after noone there came a gally
from the enymy called the Lyon wyth his flag of trewce, in
whome Don Diego de Mendoza a cavallyer of Malta and
brothers son to the Duke of Infantasgo, the Conde de Ribadeo
Don Antonio de Veltrasio, a son to the now viceroy of Peru,

146

capttayn Pedro de Vergas, and other gentyllmen [*from*] wyth
letters from Don Juan de Puertocarrero, to treate wyth the
generalls for exchandg of prysoners for such Inglysh captaynes
as weare in the gallyes and els wheare, whych was agreed on
eyther partye after the departure of these spanish gentyllmen Sir
John Wingfyld was solemly buryed in the Cathedrall church of
Cales. In his office of camp Mr. Sr Christopher Blunt suceded: in
his regiment Sr Oratio Veare, and in his shyp the Vanguard Sr
Robert Mansell

27. Sonday in the after noone the Lordes generalls dyd knight those
gentyllmen whose names insew
Don Chrystophero Prynce of Portugall
Robert Earle of Sussex
Conte Lodwyck of Nassau
Wyllm Lord Herbert
Richard Lord Burke

f.355 verso

Sr Wyllm Howard
Sr Georg Devereux
Sr Henry Neuell
Sr Edwyn Riche
Sr [blank] Levan
    netherlander
Sr [blank] [*Egem*] Aguemort
    netherlander
Sr Antony Ashlye
Sr Henry Leonard
Sr Rychard Lewson
Sr Oratio Veare
Sr Arthur Throgmorton
Sr myles Corbett
Sr Edward Conway
Sr Olyver Lambert
Sr Antony Cooke
Sr John Townesend
Sr Christopher Hayden
Sr francis Popham

Sr Phylyp Woodhouse
Sr Alexander Clyfford
Sr Moryce Barkely
Sr Charles Blont
Sr George Gyfford
Sr Robert Cross
Sr James Scudamore
Sr Uryas Lee
Sr John Lee
Sr Rychard Westen
Sr Rychard Waynman
Sr James Wotton
Sr Rychard Ruddall
Sr Robert Mansell
Sr Wyllm Monson
Sr [blank] Bowlles
Sr Edward Bowes
Sr Humphrey Drewell

f.356

Sr Amyas Preston

Sr Robert Remington

Sr John Buck

Sr John Morgan

Sr John Alderidge

Sr John Shelton

Sr Wyllm̃ Ashenden

Sr mathew Browne

Sr Thomas Ackton

Sr Thomas Gates

Sr Gylly Meryck

Sr Thomas Smyth

Sr wyllm Pooley

Sr Thomas Palmer

Sr John Stafford

Sr Wyllm Lovell

Sr John Gylbert

Sr wyllm Harvye

Sr Gerard Harvye

Sr Alexander Radcliffe

Sr Robert Dudley

28 Monday the Lordes generalls knyghted Sr wyllm Hervy and towardes evening at the mr. of the ordinances lodging a consultation was held uppon the former proposytion whether the towne was fytt to be held or no having suffycient meanes to leave vittayle to mayntayne fyve thousand men for foure monthes, by the selected cownsell it was agreed that it was fytt to be held bycawse in thatt tyme suffycient meanes of suply might be made the lordes generalls them selves in their owne shypes wyth the weakest of the fleete should retorne for England, the Lord Thomas Howard and Sr walter

f.356 verso

Raleigh wyth forty of the best shypes of warr should go to the Ilandes to ly for the Indyan fleete, to this consultation when the selected cownsell had delyvered there opinyons, /unto/ the coronells, of the Army, weare called in, and made acquaynted wyth this proiect whereunto they weare required to delyver there censures by the generall [opinion] /consent/ of them all, the former opinion was confyrmed. butt in conclusion the Lord generall Essex [discussed] albeit he agreed in opinion wyth all the rest for the holding of the cyttie yet discentyed from the same onles hym self might be left in the gard of itt, protesting thatt he would quyth him self all blame if harme or danger [should] wch he profysed would hapen to the Army if him self weare absent, but /if/ he might remayne wyth the garryson, all harmes and danger should lyght uppon him self—his reasons weare that his absence would be the cause of there ruine for that his credytt he feared would not be suffycient to send them suplyes, whereas his presence would undowtedly assure present success. This being by his lordship protested, /every man chandged his opinion, and by generall consent/ [*against whych every man discentyd by generall*] it was concluded that it was fytt to abandon the towne.

29. Tewsday they contynewed in the towne ransackinge the base pylladge of all sortes

30. Weddnisday after sonn sett the lord generall essex the Lord Marshall and most of the gentyllmen of the Army wyth 29 companies of foote and one cornett of horse wythout sound of Drom made heade into the Iland towardes the brydge for no other end but to see what contenance the enimy did hold about a myle short of the castell neare to the

f.357

brydge the Army made halt, and drew forth 300 foote som what nerer the castell to ly in ambuscado to cutt of such as should sallye forth of the castell. This night in Cales Sr George Carew mr. of the ordinance had the chardge of the Town the Lord Admirall beinge aborde the shypes

July1 Thursday morning by breake of day serteyn lose soldyers were sent to burne howses close by the Castell in hope to draw forth part of the gard wythin our Ambuscado, butt the enymie [*discr*] eyther for feare or in discretion made no sally, the Earle of Essex being in the heade of his cornett, whyche weare about 60: lances: leaving his Army where they made halt, came wythin shott of the castell gyving them many bravados to procure them to skyrmish, butt nothing could provoke them to skyrmish or to one to make a shott from the walles: whereupon the Earle retrayted to his forces and so to the towne, and on the way gave the Honor of knighthood to Mr Gray and to [*mr Ratclyff.*] In this meane tyme the Nonperylly the vangard and the Raynbow, the Mary Rose with other shypes, weare comanded by the Lord Admirall to weigh, and to feight wyth the kinges Gallyes [*the*] whych proudly came from Rota and came to the mouth of the

Bay of Cales butt /when/ [er] our shyppes [could] /weare/ come near them wythout entrering shott, /and certeyn peces discharged whych kylled dyvers of their men./ the wynd being so bare as we could make no way they fled making all possible hast along the coast towardes St Lucar. After the retorne of the Lord Generall essix to the towne he gave the Honor of knighthood to Captain Bauldwyn Merkyrk Srgeant maior of his Regiment, and to Captayn Gerrard Hervy being bothe wonded at the surpryse of Cales

2. fryday being the uttermost day requested by the prysoners for the payment of the 120/n/. ducates not being then come the 50 prysoners thatt weare in pledg for itt weare distrybuted amongst the shypes.

### f.357 verso

3. Saterday the Lordes stayed [in the towne] /yett in Cales/ expectynge the payment of the 120/n/ crownes aforesaid butt the mony came not: 2: messingers only weare sent from the Duke de Medena one a [deletion] Cannon of Cales, the other a gentyllman of Xeres called Matteo Marques di Gaetano to the generalls to intreate them to deliver the prisoners, and to accept marchantes bylls and bondes for the payment thereof whych was by the lordes refused Captain [cap] fishborne who was left at Plymouth by reason of the leake wch was in the Jonas came to us to Cales bringing wyth hym a carvell, and had a bord hym Captayn Collyer and his companie

4 Sonday morning, order was given for the imbarking of all the Army [according the] by regiments the first that was shypped weare the Regimentes of Sr Oratio Veare /who had Sr John Wyngfyld regiment/ and Sr.Rychard Wingfyld, then the regimentes of Sr Conyers Clyfford and Sr Thomas Gerrard & after them the regiments of Sr Christopher Blunt and the Earle of Sussex and lastly the regimentes of the Lord Marshall and the Lord Generall Essex, wch tow regimentes weare uppon the gard of the port of the towne to the land ward, untyll the rest weare imbarked, and of them all drawne away butt 300. wch weare of his Ld: regiment only: who stayed uppon thatt /gard/ to the last and weare shypped by the Lord Generall Essex hym self who accompanied wyth dyvers great officers and /sondry/ gentyllmen

of the Army stayed to see the last man abord. by thatt the tow first regimentes weare imbarked the towne was begon to be fyred wch left not burning in our vew untyll weddnesday night following at wch tyme we lost sight thereof. moreover this night all the syck and hurte in the Army weare selected from the rest and dispersed with shypes apointed for thatt purpose to make there present retorne into Ingland. And further the Hollanders Ryding farthest into the bay sent certeyn companyes a shore towards the castell fast by the brydge at sight of whose aproch the enymye abandoned the forte, and the Hollanders burnt it to the grownd, as that castell excepted, the hole Iland was formerly burnt by the Lord general Essex on /the/ Thursday before. In all this tyme of our being in Cales wch was 14 dayes, albeit the

f.358

enimy was gathered to a head at Syvyll Xeres Port St Mary Port Reall to an army of about 50/n/ strong yett in this tyme we never had alarum eyther by land or sea to disturbe, but lyved in as greatt tranquyllytie and ease as if we had beene in cheap syde. this night we wayde Anker and upon bordes freed our selves out of the Bay into the Roade where we ankered.

5. Monday in the after noone a gally was sent from Don Juan de Puertocarrero: who brought letters from hym and the marques St Croce to the Lord Admirall, wyth 39: Inglish captyne, for exchandge of so many of there nation wch was assented unto, and accordingly exchandg made. The rest of the Inglish Captynes at Cyvyll and St Lucar weare lykewyse promysed to be sent forthwyth uppon lyke condytions this gally in her coming into our fleete being then under sale over against Rota from whence she carryed so small a flag of trewce as it could hardly be discerned was shott at by one of our small barkes and kylled tow [of his] or thre men

6. Tewsday the wynd so bare as we dyd not pas Rota 2: leages from Cales

7. weddnisday aboute 10: a clocke athwarte of Chyppiona 2 fleebotes bownd for Cales and laden wyth deale bordes as far /as is/ yett known [wear] fell in to our fleete, whereof the one was taken, and the other by the goodnes of hys sale, gott into the Barr of St Lucar:

8. Thursday calmes and bare wyndes so as all the day we gayned lyttle in our corse

9. fryday the Generalls met abord the Arke wheare it was agreed that we should land our forces at Aymonte from thence to pas over the water to Castro marin then to marche to Tanylla, and so to faro: also the same day sr Antony Ashly in the Lyons whelpe was dispatched to the court of England

### f.358 verso

and for that the Earle of Sussex was fallen syck /wch [after] proved of the missels/ and desirous to retorne for England Sr Robert Cross in the Swyftsure was commanded to transporte hym, also wyth these shypes Sr Gylly Meryck, and about 14: sale more of Hoyes [and] fleebotes [wyth] and small barkes wyth Horses sick men and pilladg had lycence to depart. [After] uppon whose departure the mr. of the Ordinance in the Marie Rose dyd beare the vyceadmiralls flag of that Squadron

10. Saterday morning the generalls for feare of being imbayd wythin the Cape of St Maries, if any thing weare attempted at Aymonte wch is to the east of the sayd cape aboute 8: leages they altered their porpose and resolved to land and water at Pharaon, a Cyttie in Algarbe and the cheefe port in it, in wch towne there is ever resident a Bishop.

11 Sonday morning before sonrysing a seabord our fleete /aleven/ of the kinges gallyes gave chase to a flybote called the Peter of Anchusen, bound for Ingland [and laden to transport sick and hurt soldyers and horses] and to a small of Plymouth aperteyning to Sr ferdinando Gorges wch towe shypes [of] weare of our [fleete], /Army/ the Peter of Anchusen wythin a leage [of] /a heade/ our fleete was taken by the gallyes and towed away: beinge impossible to rescu her by reason of the deade calme: but the small man of Plymouth escaped, they being affrayed to spend longer tyme in the wch our shypes might come up unto them: in this flyboate we lost [of] /hurt and syck/ soldyers and mariners, inglish and flemish, about 120: persons and sondry horses aperteyning to the Lord Thomas Howard, the mr. of the Ordinance etc: and some pilladge of good valew

12. Monday morning the Lord Thomas Howard wyth aboute 40

saile [*of*] in his companie, whome we had lost 4: dayes before was descryed to sterne us to the east ward who before night came into our fleete. Also this day Sir Bauldwin Merkyrk srgeant maior of the Lord Generall Essex his regiment who was hurt as aforesayd at the winning of Cales dyed of his wownd, was buryed in sea /close along the shore/ a lyttle to the westward of of the Cape St Maries. And towardes night [*we have rain*] having having a styff gale of wynd from the shore we bare Rome into the sea

### f.359

13. Tewsday morning we made into the land, and before tenn a clocke the hole fleete came to Anker before the mowth of the /westerly/ creeke [*to the westerly:*] of the Haven of Pharo[*n*] and wyth all possible expedityon bothe the Lordes Generalls and the hole Army weare disimbarked and landed upon [*and*] the pointe of land opposite to the Iland whose easterly point is the Cape St. Mary: The heate of the day being very extreme, the Lord Admirall whose yeares and bodye unfytt for travaile, and especially in this [*hote*] clyment, was so distempered wyth the heat as by the intrety of the Lord Generall Essex and others contrary to his desires, retorned to his shypes: [*by*] /after/ sonn setting the hole Army began to marche, and incamped aboute a good /myle/ into the country: [*wheare*]

14. Weddnisdaye at the discharginge of the watch the Vanguard led by Sr Christopher Blunt whose regiment had the point, began to marche: the hole Army followed Ranged into 18: Battayliones the Earle hym self fyndinge the gentyllmen /adventurers whose names insew/ ranged in the front of the vanguard left his horse, and led the same hym self on whome besides the Coronell and Captaynes of the Regiment the Prynce of Portugall, the Lord Thomas Howard, and the mr. of the Ordinance attended. In our marche we saw no enimie to make resistance, and all thatt we sawe weare few horse and foote scattered uppon hylls to vew our troopes. aboutt 12. a clocke the vangard entered into the Cyttye of faro beinge distant from our landing above thre leages, wheare the inhabytantes weare fled /wyth their goodes/ in so muche as hardely any person could be fownd and the houses left bare and naked. The Lord General quartered hym self in the Bishopes

howse The names of these gentyllmen adventurers thatt bare pykes and marched in the front of the Vanguard led by the Lord Generall

f.359 verso [blank]

f.360

15 Thursday by breake of Day the mr. of the Ordinance hys companie by order from the Lord Generall on way and Captain Sr Clement Heigham Captain Brett and Captain Upsher wyth certein troupes compownded of all the companies to the number of sixhundreth, marched another way into the contry towardes the montaynes, and before night all retorned having burnt /manie/ [the] villadges and howses, wyth cattell and other good pylladge: in this march dyvers of our men wyth dronkenes fayntenes and scattering weare cutt of by the enymie, who ever more weare in sight, butt never durst chardge the troupes. Also the same day Don Juan de Puertocarrero, wrotte unto the Lord Admirall for the relesing of Don Diego Cabezza de Vacca prisoner of Sr Bauldwin Merkyrk deceased. The gallyes by hym sent wyth this message /who came with a flag of trewce/ came to Anker in the mydle of the Iland of the Cape St Marye [in the mydst of] /betwene/ our fleete, wch weare at Anker at eyther end of the Iland that leadeth to faro: butt uppon the admonition of the Lord Admirall /by cause they weare uppon his safe conduct/ they quytted there Ankeridge, and made out into the sea. by these messingers we had intelligence that the Peter of Anchusen, whych was taken the Sonday afore as aforesaide, before such tyme as she had yelded she lost 30: of her own companie and slew forty of the enimye by a trayne of powder, thatt blew them up [at] when they weare entered.

16. frydaye by mischance a dutch Captaine and of good estymation amongst them, was by a soldyer of Captain Talkerns in the merkett slayne wyth the blow of muskett for wch fact by the marshalls court he was adiuged to [dye] /be shott to death/ uppon whome about four aclocke the hole Army being in the markett place execution was don and imedyatly the vanguard marched towardes the water syde and before fowre a clocke the reare gard

led by the Lord Generall hym self was drawne forth [*of*] leaving the towne burnt to the growND. This night we incamped againe wheare we lodged after our landinge

17. Saterday before 4: a clocke in the after noone the hole Army was imbarked againe whych Don the Generalls and selected cownsell met abord the Arke, wheare a consultation was held what was fytt to be don by our Army before our retorne into England, wheare every mans opinion was [*herd*] demanded and herd, butt nothing concluded, butt referred to a second meting

### f.360 verso

18 Sonday morning the Lords Generalls /and Cownsell/ mett abord the Repulse wheare after lardge debating, it was agreed thatt the hole fleete should not make stay or water in any place untyll we came to the Rocke in the mowth of the Ryver of Lysbona, and there to consider [*for*] wat further should be don. wch don [*we weighed*] having a leading wynde we sett sale.

19:[*20*] Monday continewed our course for cape St Vincent, the winde not beinge very lardge

20: Tewsday about one a clocke in the after noone we dobled the Cape St Vincent, wythin sacre shott of the shore wyth a franke wynd at the last, butt we had not sayled fowre leages to the northward of the Cape, butt we mett wyth the land breese whych dyd over blow and carryed us into the sea

21.22. weddnisdaye and Thursdaye dry and stormy, continewing constantly at North.

23 fryday towardes the after noone the storme was fully spent and the Lordes Generalls abord the Arke hunge forth a flag of the Queenes Armes, whereupon the selected cownsell mett [*there*] where it was concluded thatt we should make for the Iland of St Mychell in the Azurres wheare a good hope was left eyther to meete wyth the East Jndian or west indian fleete, assured meanes to water, whereof the fleete had greate wont and the Iland in it self rich. butt if we should happely mete wyth a strong westerly wynd in so much as uppon no bord we could recover the Ilandes then the porpose was to go for Ingland, at this cownsell was lykewyse dyspatched into Ingland the Centurion the Elyzabeth, the Gyft of god, the George of London the Jacob of Roterdam,

the Peter [*of*] and the Jacob of Anchusen wyth certain hoyes of horses

24 Saterday the winde came aboute to the west, and west south west, in so much as wyth that wind there was no course to hold to the Ilandes, whereupon these shypes formerly dismissed for Ingland, weare stayed, and the fleete bore

### f.361

to the Northwardes. In whych course, by reason of fowle wether the fleete was wonderfully scattered

25. Sondaye the styff gale contynewed in the wych the fleete gathered together againe

26. Monday morning A flag of the Queenes Armes was hung forth of the Arke, whereuppon the cownsell assembled, the questions [*was*] debated was to understand whether it weare more fytt to ly for the retorne of the Carrykes, or to dyrect our course for Ingland the opinion of the maior part if a competent fleete vittaled might be selected out of the Navye that it weare fytt to ly of and on uppon the hight of the Rock untyll the retorne of the Carryckes, butt finding an imposibitye to rayse such a fleete as aforesayde it was concluded by the Generall assent of all, that we should stand for the Northerly Cape called Cape finisterre, and then to putt in for the Groyne if upon discovery it should be fownd that any shypes of the kinges weare in that harborow.

27. Tewsday the day faire lyttle wynd butt thatt whych was, fytt for our course. after sonn sett a styff gale arose from west south west wch contynewed all that night

28 Weddnesdaye towardes the eveninge a storme of wind and rayne arose, in the whych the Earle of Essex, having the war spyte, the vangard wyth other shyppes not exceding 20 sale in his company continewing there course lost the Lord Admirall and the rest of the fleete who imedyatly uppon the setting of the sonn tacked aboute and bare Rome into the sea

### f.361 verso

29. Thursday the day calmy and fayre

30. fryday morning aboute 8. of clock uppon a starbord bow we made the north cape comonly called Cape finisterre and before

tenn a clocke [*und*] far of under our lee, neare to the shore we
discryed the Earle wyth the shypes whych weare on Weddnisday
lost. towardes night bycause we weare not able to doble the Cape
on that borde, the hole fleete bare Rome to the sea. this evening
the Lord Generall wyth his shypes fell into the fleete

31.Saterday the day faire, [*wy*] the wind lardge in so much as er
night we had dobled the northerly cape and weare a thwart of
Monicy: this daye, west mr of the Mary Rose by the Lord
Admralls direction was sent in a Carvayle to discover whatt
shyping Ryd wythin the Harborow at the Groyne.

August first Sonday morning by 8: a clocke we came before the
entrance of the Haven of the Groyne, wheare the Carvayle
dispatched the day before retorned unto us wyth the report thatt
in those harborows there was no shypping whereuppon a flag of
Cownsell was hung forth, and the Lords and Cownsell mett
abord the Arke, wheare it was resolved we should forthwyth
direct our course for Ingland upon consideration that there was
not in the Groyne or faroff at that present any shypping. and also
in regard there was great want of vittall in the fleete, in so much
as the most weare not vittalled for above 14. dayes as the weake
of estate the fleete was in by reason of sicknes. This daye abord
the Arke the Admyrall of Holland called Sr John de van vorde
dyd resave by the Lordes Generalls joyntly the Honor of
Knyghthoode

### f.362

Also Sr walter Raleigh in regarde of the great sicknes that was
abord his shyp obteyned leave to make the best hast he could to
Plymouth wyth hym there weare dispatched, wyth letters to the
Queene and Cownsell from the Lordes Generalls. Sr Arthure
Savadge, Sr Edward Conway and mr George Buck Buck was
dispatched wyth the report that our porpose was to go for the
Ilandes, and there to attend the Carryckes and bare date the
[blank] July. Sr Arthur Savadge was dispatched wyth our
porpose to leave the course towardes the Ilandes and to make for
the Groyne and bare date the [blank] of July. Sr Edward Conway
was to make relation what we fownd at the Groyne, and our
porpose to [*reter*] make for Ingland. as also to know her m/ties/

plesure what her wyll is should be don wyth this Army. whether
it shall be cashered or no. wyth Sr walter Raleigh, the Ro Buck
and the John and francis were dysmyssed

2. Monday the affectyon and St. Tos: mr watts shyppes being
vittaled wyth a proportion above the rest of the fleete obteyned
leave of the Lordes Generalls to retorne for the Cape, wyth
porpose to ly of and on to spend the remaynder of the provisions
in hope to gett porchase: all the day calmes

3. Tewsdaye & monday calmy.

4. Weddnisday the wind became good and blew in a styff gale
westerly whereby, [whether,] by the storme, and by their desires
homeward every [do] one taking his owne course the fleete was
dispersed and scattered

5 Thursday the wind good and they held on there courses for
Ingland.

### f.362 verso

6. Saturday /fryday/ the Lord Thomas Howard and Sr. walter
Raleigh came into the sound of Plymouth. the Mirhonor being in
greate danger to have bene sonke by the abondance of water
whych was in, by reason of a leak whych by no meanes they could
stop nor hardly by pomping preserve from sinking

7 Saterday the Lord Admirall wyth the gros of the fleete came into
the Sound of Plymouth wch daye the Earle of Essex, in the
Repulse, Sr George Carewe in the Mary Rose, the flemish
squadron and the remaynder of the fleete made the Lysard,
being the first part of Ingland that was discovered.

8 Sonday the Lord Generall Essex wyth the rest came into the
Sound of Plymouth, being thatt day tenn weekes of the Lordes
shypping there at Plymouth.

# Appendix II

Journal of Jan van Doornik
concerning the expedition to Cadiz in the
year 1596 from an MS. in the Imperial Library
in Vienna.
(Dates given are those of the
Gregorian calendar, not, as in Sir George
Carew, from the Julian calendar.)

Voyage done with my kinsman Van Warmont, Admiral of Holland, to the assistance of the Queen of England, in the year 1596, when she had equipped a beautiful armada, which was commanded by the Earl of Essex and milord Charles Hauwart, chief admiral of England, etc.

Having been accepted on the 10th of April by the Admirality of Amsterdam, sailed from there on the 15th and lay before Jacob Hanness to await the tides.

Lifted anchor in the evening and came to Pampes in the night.
16. Passed Pampes
18. Arrived in Texel, and there a review was held by representatives of the Admirality.
23. Towards evening, the wind at North-East by North, sailed out with a small breeze.
25. Arrived at Flushing and having there found the ships anchored that had come out of the Maas, and those which were fitted out in Zeeland.
29. Where his Excellency came to examine the ship and stayed as guest for the afternoon meal.

## MAY
1st Sailed in the morning at daybreak, wind North-East, and still arrived the same evening off England.

2nd Came through the Heads [Forelands], wind Northerly, and proceeded South-West by West.

3rd Passed near Portland, proceeded West by North.

4. Arrived in the harbour of Plymouth to await the whole fleet. Anchored in the Cattegat.

9. The Earl of Essex came overland from the court, and inspected the whole fleet with my kinsman.

11. The chief Admiral arrived with 12 large ships and also inspected the fleet.

12. Was at Saltaes [Saltash] which is a proper little village, lying three English miles up the river. Saw there the ship with which Thomas Candisch [Cavendish] made his last trip to the Straits of Magellan, whereabouts he died.

23. Experienced a heavy storm from the North North-East and which drove a pinnace coming in on to the rocks.

## JUNE

8. The wind from the North North-West, the fleet took on board two regiments of foot-soldiers.

9. The wind North West with showers, took another regiment on board.

10. Warped out of the harbour, wind West North-North-West.

11. Dropped anchor in the roadstead outside, the wind at North North-West sailed with the sun at South West, at sea the wind became West.

12. The wind remaining westerly, again arrived at Plymouth with the sun South.

13. Again set sail with the whole fleet, the wind North West, the sun South East.

14. The wind North North-West continued South West and having arrived in the morning in the channel awaited some ships and proceeded again with a South West sun.

15. We had calm with wind West South-West, having turned West, we shot 48 1/3 [latitude] in the evening turned and proceeded West and West by South.

16. During the night proceeded with a North West wind.

17. Shot 47 1/2 about half-way in the Spanish sea.

18. Shot 46 precisely, the wind northerly.

19. Shot 45 1/6, proceeded South-West by South.
20. During the night went South South-West and South-West by South the wind North West, shot 44 1/4 degrees.
21. At 43 degrees, at the height of Cape Finisterre, the wind North by West we were at a guess 28 leagues off land, in the afternoon shot 42 1/3 degrees. At night got the wind at North North-East with clear weather.
22nd Shot 41 degrees, the wind North North-East and proceeded South-East by South.
23. Came opposite the Berlingas, which are five rocks situated near the river of Lisbon, on one of which there used to be a monastery which was destroyed by the English a long time ago, with the wind at North North-East we proceeded South East, and in the evening southwardly. When we were at the longitude of St Vuschoeck [sic], there were English pinnaces gone to the shore which brought a barque to the fleet in the evening.
24. Proceeded South by East and saw the Vijgenberch [Fig Mountain], the wind North.
25. Sighted Cape St. Vincent and Cape St. Maria, the wind having turned East North-East and proceeded South East. Today a Flushing man was held by the English who had been attacked twice and besides him two other Dutchmen who took from the two ships 370,000 guilders; what they took from a third ship, which came from Middelburgh, is not yet known.
26. The wind East blown hither and thither, we sailed past Cape St. Maria.
26. Tacked and lost more than we gained.
28. A quiet day, and in the evening a cool breeze from the West. The same day an Irishman was caught by the English, who came from Cadiz, and who said there were 35 or 36 ships in that bay. The cool breeze continued during the night.
29. The wind still westerly, but quiet.
30. Sighted Cadiz early in the morning, had a cool breeze till evening, did nothing but having tacked to and fro for some time, dropped anchor in the mouth of the bay, in which were discovered lying at anchor 8 galleons, 3 frigates, 18 galleys, and 34 Indian merchantmen, against which the English had fired some shots from afar, being next to them. It appears that the

English had decided to land at St. Catalina that day. But as the Admiral with this in mind had manned his sloop, most of the people in her were drowned by the wind. As a result of this and as the Spaniards buried them in the aforementioned place and as further landing was difficult, they changed their mind.

## JULY

1st  The majority of the merchantmen retired inwards to the Creek of Port Real, the galleys remaining lying at the City, but being severely damaged by our incoming ships which one after another as they sailed past the town ran into the bay, they retired to the bridge of Herod, excepting two which, shot out of action, remained till they were somewhat equipped again and then, having been well supplied by the burghers, towards evening sailed seawards.

The galleons with the best equipped Indiamen had put themselves across the bay at the Punctael to await us there, against which on our side were set seven or eight of the largest vessels and the shooting from both sides lasted about 3 to 4 hours.

At about South Eastern sun one of our ships exploded, as it seems because the ammunition was badly stored, and the Captain Lieutenant and about 50 men were killed. The Captain Pilot and about 20 men were saved.

Meanwhile the shooting continued on both sides, but more intense from our side, and hit St. Philip, Spanish Admiral, who seeing that he was being deserted by his (first eleven strong) ships, who all made course inwards, fired at them, but not being able to stop them with these methods, finally cut the cable, and stranded off the Punctael, about two o'clock, because besides the firing of the others, three Dutch ships tried to board him.

When the ship was stranded the men left the ship in disorder to get to land first (alas, not all) leaving four with the gunpowder and to care for the wounded. Because as our sailors were preparing to climb to get the flag from above, fire came into the ship and the ropes, and shortly after it exploded without doing more damage than to sink an English pinnace, which was lying so close near it that it could not be salvaged, the men of which were taken into one of the Dutch ships.

The Vice-Admiral St. Thomas with St. Mark got into the hands of the English and taken to England.

The ships having been taken the [allies'] men were put on land, helped by the firing of some of the ships of the fleet of small draught, as some Spaniards on horseback showed themselves from time to time, coming from the dunes. The English having landed divided into two groups, the one going to the bridge [of Suaco] to take it, the other to the city, which they captured after a few skirmishes, arriving at the gates pell mell with the Spaniards with very little loss of life only 60 men.

Before the English landed (who alone were ordered to do so) Jan Garbrantsz, Vice-Admiral of the Hollanders went on land with 14 men and took the Punctael, from which the garrison had fled, even though there were four cannon on it, and was thus the first to put foot on land, and raised the flag of the Prince.

Having arrived in the City, they occupied the Town Hall, where some were killed, and as night was falling, on account of which the Earl of Essex did not proceed, but stayed in it fortifying it and putting things in order for the approaching day.

2. The bulwark commanding the Caye, called St. Philip, surrendered, paying 20,000 ducats for life and goods, as also La Villa or the old town for 120,000 ducats, from where men conveyed to the bridge all who wished, further plundering all that had not been found on them.

The same day the Corregidor attended the Chiefs to treat with them about the ransom for the Indiamen and would have agreed to two million if it had not happened that they were seen put on fire by order of the Duke of St. Lucar [Medina Sidonia].

Later the Corregidor and the Provedor affirmed that the fleet was worth 12 million, according to the estimate when they were brought in for toll.

Today one saw the Indiamen burn fiercely to the sorrow of the merchants.

4. Have still plundered, and some people transferred to Port Real.

5th These people then came with galleys and also barques with consent to make a treaty concerning the prisoners and other matters.

6. And Afterwards visited the wrecks and took from them all kinds of goods.

7. After the sermon in the cloister of St. Francis more than 50 Knights were created by the Earl of Essex among whom was Count Louis of Nassau.

10th During the night our boats having sailed to the wrecks found there Spaniards, decided on a plan, have agreed that ours would first load to capacity and thereafter the Spaniards; which took place in good faith.

14. The City was fired in many quarters.

# Appendix III

## TONNAGE MEASUREMENTS

It was once commonly, but mistakenly, believed that Elizabethan men-of-war were smaller and handier than those of Spain, an error arising from a difference in their standards of measurement. Since the fourteenth century the wine trade between England and France had used large casks of standard size, tun in English, 2,240 lb. (1,016 kg.), and *tonneau* in French, 2,000 *livres* (979 kg.). These figures were based on the weight of the casks when filled with wine. Vessels were said to be of so many tons according to the number of casks they could carry, and, allowing for wastage in fitting round containers into ships' holds, one ton equalled 60 cubic feet. This medieval standard was carried over into the ocean trade. In Spain the corresponding unit was the *tonelada* and early in the sixteenth century 1 ton, 1 *tonneau de mer* and 1 *tonelada* were about equal. Port authorities all over Europe sought to standardise these measurements for three reasons, to assess harbour dues, to gauge accurately the draught of a fully loaded vessel, and to avoid overloading. (The Venetians had the equivalent of a Plimsoll line in the thirteenth century.) In wartime, however, captains tended to state tonnage at a figure well above the true one in order to claim higher compensation if they were requisitioned for naval service. When, for example, a privately owned ship was taken into Philip II's navy, it was paid for at twenty per cent more than its peace-time tonnage. During his long reign capacities registered in *toneladas* were gradually lowered, so that 500 *toneladas* in 1550 was the equivalent of 350 in 1600. For example, in the Armada fight the English captured the *San Salvador*, registered in Spain as 953 *toneladas*, and found that by English measurement she was only 600 tons.

# CALENDAR OF ENGLISH SHIPS
## NAMED IN THE *MARY ROSE* JOURNAL

| Ships | Built/ Rebuilt | Tons | Guns (in pounds weight of shot fired) | | | | | | | | | | |
|---|---|---|---|---|---|---|---|---|---|---|---|---|---|
| | | | 60 | 34 | 32 | 30 | 18 | 9 | 8 | 6 | 4 | Other | Total |
| Affection | | 120 | | | | | | | | | | | |
| Alcedo | | 400 | | | | | | | | | | | |
| Answer | 1590 | 200 | | | | | | 5 | 8 | 2 | 6 | | 21 |
| Ark Royal | 1587 | 694 | 4 | | | 4 | | 12 | 12 | 6 | | 17 | 55 |
| Centurion | | 300 | | | | | | | | | | | |
| Charles | | 80 | | | | | | | | | | | |
| Crane | 1590 | 253 | | | | | | 6 | | 7 | 6 | 5 | 24 |
| Dreadnought | 1573 | 450 | 2 | | | | 4 | 11 | | 10 | | 14 | 41 |
| Due Repulse | 1596 | 777 | | | | | | | | | | | 48 |
| Elizabeth | | | | | | | | | | | | | |
| Falcon | | 100 | | | | | | | | | | | 15 |
| George | | 100 | | | | | | | | | | | |
| Gift of God | | 80 | | | | | | | | | | | |
| John & Francis | | | | | | | | | | | | | |
| Jonas | | 60 | | | | | | | | | | | |

# Appendix IV

| Men | Commander | Master | Remarks |
|---|---|---|---|
| | | | Owned by Sir John Watts, the leading promoter of privateering<br>Privateered for Earl of Cumberland in 1598 |
| 135 | | | Owned by Sir John Watts<br>Privateered for Earl of Cumberland in 1598 |
| | | | Queen's ship |
| 380 | Howard of Effingham | W. Jones | *Queen's ship, built at Deptford for Raleigh and sold to the Queen |
| 80 | | | Owned by Thomas Cordell<br>Privateered for the City of London in 1591 & for the Earl of Cumberland in 1598 |
| 45 | Sackvill Trevor | Edmond Musgrave | *Queen's ship. Privateered for Howard of Effingham in 1591 |
| 95 | Sir Robert Mansell (suc. by Jonas Bradbury) | Matthew Woodcott | Queen's ship |
| 180 | Sir Alex. Clifford | James Beare | *Queen's ship built at Deptford |
| 340 | Earl of Essex | Thomas Grove | Queen's ship |
| | | | Probably the Elizabeth sent by Raleigh with other ships to colonise Virginia in 1585 |
| | | | Queen's ship. Sailed to Newfoundland with Gilbert and Raleigh in 1578 |
| | | | Possibly Queen's ship |
| | | | Privateered in 1591 |
| | | | Privateered for John More, Thomas Cordell & others in 1598 |
| | Capt. Fishborne | | |

# THE COUNTER-ARMADA, 1596

| Ships | Built/ Rebuilt | Tons | 60 | 34 | 32 | 30 | 18 | 9 | 8 | 6 | 4 | Other | Total |
|---|---|---|---|---|---|---|---|---|---|---|---|---|---|
| Lion | 1582 | 500 | | 4 | | | 8 | 14 | | 9 | | 25 | 60 |
| Lioness | | | | | | | | | | | | | |
| Lion's Whelp | | 90 | | | | | | | | | | | |
| Mary Rose | 1589 | 600 | | 4 | | | 11 | 10 | | | | 14 | 39 |
| Mere Honour | 1590 | 709 | | 4 | | | 15 | 16 | | 4 | | 2 | 41 |
| Moon | 1586 | 85 | | | | | | | | 4 | 4 | 1 | 9 |
| Nonpareil | 1589 | 600 | 2 | 3 | | | 7 | 8 | | 12 | | 24 | 56 |
| Quittance | 1590 | 257 | | | | | 2 | 6 | | 7 | 4 | 6 | 25 |
| Rainbow | 1586 | 384 | | 6 | | | 12 | 7 | | 1 | | | 26 |
| Roebuck | | 240 | | | | | | | | | | | |
| St Thomas | | | | | | | | | | | | | |
| Swan | | 250 | | | | | | | | | | | |
| Swiftsure | 1573 | 80 | | | | | | | | | | | 42 |
| Tremontana | 1586 | 150 | | | | | | | | 12 | 7 | 2 | 21 |
| True Love | | | | | | | | | | | | | |
| Vanguard | 1586 | 450 | | | 4 | | 14 | 11 | | 2 | | | 31 |
| Warspite | 1596 | 648 | 2 | 2 | | | 13 | 10 | | 2 | | 11 | 40 |

| Men | Commander | Master | Remarks |
|---|---|---|---|
| 245 | Sir Robert Southwell | W. Parsey | *Queen's ship. Privateered in West Indies 1591 |
| 105 | | | |
| 45 | Capt. William King | | Queen's ship. Privateered for Howard of Effingham in 1590 & Howard & Robert Sadler in 1598 |
| 245 | Sir George Carew | Thomas West | *Queen's ship |
| 390 | Lord Thomas Howard | John Hankyn | Queen's ship |
| 40 | Henry Moyle | Robert Kelly | *Queen's ship |
| 245 | Sir Robert Dudley | John Endycke | *Queen's ship |
| 95 | Sir George Gifford | Thomas Tenant | Queen's ship |
| 240 | Sir William Monson | John Grey | *Queen's ship |
| 104 | | | Privateered for Thomas Cavendish 1590/91. With him on his last voyage 1595. Sent by Raleigh with other ships to colonise Virginia in 1585 |
| | | | Owned by Sir John Watts |
| | Sir Richard Weston | | Taken by Essex for Cadiz though about to sail against Portuguese colonies |
| 180 | Sir Robert Cross | J. Whiskynges | *Queen's ship. Privateered for George Raymond 1589 |
| | William King | William Coste | *The name means North Wind |
| 70 | Sir Richard Leveson | J. Manne | Privateered for Howard of Effingham and Sir Robert Cecil in 1598 |
| 240 | Sir John Wingfield (suc. by Sir Robert Mansell) | James Woodcott | *Queen's ship |
| 290 | Sir Walter Raleigh | Robert Hankyn | Queen's ship |
| | | | *Known to have sailed against the Spanish Armada, 1588 |

# Appendix V

## PORTRAITS OF SIR GEORGE CAREW, FIRST EARL OF TOTNES

Sir George Carew was created Baron Carew of Clopton, near Stratford-on-Avon, his wife's family home, in 1605, when he was Vice-Chamberlain to James I's queen, Anne of Denmark. In 1626, following the accession of Charles I, he was created Earl of Totnes in Devon. Two large portraits of him, painted in old age, are extant, one at Gorhambury, the country seat of the Earls of Verulam near St. Albans, and the other in the National Portrait Gallery in London. They appear to be two versions of the same picture. Both show him standing bareheaded, wearing a cuirass over his doublet; his right hand rests on the top of a walking stick, the left on the hilt of his sword. His contemporary, Edward Somerset, Earl of Worcester, whose portrait is also at Gorhambury, is seen in a similar pose, and the frames of the two pictures bear the name of the same artist, George Geldorp, a well-known portraitist, who, before he came to London in the 1620's, was a member of the painters' guild in Antwerp and a friend of Van Dyck.

Though no painting of Sir George as a young man has yet been recognised, there are certain peculiarities in the features visible in both the National Portrait Gallery and Gorhambury pictures which, taken together, would make reasonably certain the identification of an earlier portrait, if one could be found. The thumb and forefinger of the right hand are remarkably long and slender; the lobe of the ear large; the eyes round and bright, though the left is noticeably less so than the right; the lips at the left corner of the mouth droop slightly, a defect that the moustache, trimmed in the fashion of forty years before, does not completely hide; the nose is long and straight; the eyebrows arched and, unlike the head hair and beard, dark, a characteristic of brows that have been red in youth.

The first place to look for a portrait of an Elizabethan courtier is among the works of the miniaturist Nicholas Hilliard. Between 1570 and 1600 there was practically nobody of any note in the Queen's entourage who did not sit to him. One of his masterpieces, formerly in the collection of Sir Hans Sloane, now at the Victoria and Albert Museum, London, is catalogued only as 'a man clasping a hand from a cloud'. It is inscribed *Attici amoris ergo Ano.Dm.1588*. The unknown subject is dressed in the height of court fashion wearing a sugar-loaf hat with a short brim and embroidered band, and a fall-down lace collar. The long, elegant thumb and finger of the right hand tenderly clasp a woman's hand reaching down from above. The symbolism is clear; he has been raised up by someone high above him in rank, and the inscription confirms this by alluding to a passage in Ovid, the Roman poet who more than any other ancient writer inspired the art and literature of the Renaissance. In it he tells how Aurora, goddess of the dawn, snatched up Cephalos, a youth of Attica, but afterwards gave him back to his wife Procris:

> '. . . cum pleno concita velo
> Attica puppis adest, in portus intrat amicos.
> Quae Cephalum patriaeque simul mandata ferebat.'[1]

This is the story to which Milton, a great admirer of the Elizabethans, alluded in *Il Penseroso*:

> 'Till civil-suited Morn appear
> Not tricked and frounced, as she was wont
> With the Attic boy to hunt . . .'

The inscription therefore means 'For Love of the Attic boy', and the hand appearing from above is that of Aurora. It does not, however, descend from a cloud. When Hilliard wished to depict cloud, he did so, as in his portrait of the Earl of Cumberland, and that of 'A youth leaning against a tree'.[2] Instead, he has drawn the cuff of a woman's sleeve. Its shell-like shapes, made of a diaphanous material, instantly recall those of the dress which the Queen is wearing in the large Armada portrait, now at Woburn

Abbey, which Hilliard is believed to have designed, though he may have left the painting to another hand. Significantly the date on the miniature is that of the Armada campaign. Moreover there is no difficulty in identifying the hand as that of Elizabeth, because Aurora was a goddess whom Elizabethan courtiers professed to see reincarnated in their Queen. In this extravagant flattery no one joined with more enthusiasm than Sir Walter Raleigh, who addressed her in a poem beginning:

> 'Now we have present made
> To Cynthia, Phoebe, Flora,
> Diana and Aurora,
> Beauty that cannot fade.'[3]

The sitter's red-gold hair half-conceals the large lobe of his ear; the nose is long and straight; the moustache scarcely hides a slight deformity at the left corner of the mouth; the left eye is less brilliant than the right; but the brows are strong and finely arched. Add all these features to the striking elegance of his fingers and thumb, and the result is not a series of random coincidences, but proof that it was Sir George Carew who sat for this jewel-like portrait, intending it to be a present for the Queen. To please her, he wore a black doublet, knowing that she preferred men to wear sombre colours. Like his cousin Raleigh, he had good reason for gratitude. From boyhood Elizabeth had shown him favour. He was already one of her Gentlemen-Pensioners and a knight when, in 1587, the office of Master of Ordnance in Ireland fell vacant through the death of his uncle, Sir Jacques Wingfield. The Lord Deputy in Ireland at once appointed his own son, but in October Sir George wrote to the Queen, claiming the post as his by right:

'Though I have no cause to mistrust your Majesty's favour, yet, being so hardly mated with an adversary so mightily friended, I hope you will pardon my bold attempt . . . I am content to submit myself to your pleasure whose incomparable virtues, accompanied by nature's rarest perfections, have been evermore by all men most worthily esteemed the world's glory and our age's wonder.'[4]

To further his case, Sir George, leaving his wife in Ireland, came to the court at Greenwich, but, the matter being still unsettled three months later, he wrote to the Earl of Leicester seeking his help:

'I have diligently attended ever since your repair into England to speak to your Lordship. The continual favour which you have ever shown to my brother and me from the time when we were servants to you and your brother, emboldens me to ask the continuance of your kindness.'[5]

As a result, in February 1588, the Queen commanded the Lord Deputy to replace his son with Sir George, who was to enjoy the Mastership 'in as ample a manner as it was held by his predecessors'.[6] The Queen had raised him up. Now was the perfect moment to present her with an appropriate gift, his portrait in miniature, inscribed with words that so excellent a Latinist would instantly recognise as an elegant expression of admiration and thanks.

### Appendix V Notes

1. Ovid, *Metamorphoses* VII 490–3.
2. Victoria and Albert Museum, London.
3. W. F. Oakeshott, *The Queen and the Poet*, 1960.
4. Carew MSS, Lambeth Palace.
5. Carew MSS, Lambeth Palace.
6. Carew MSS, Lambeth Palace.

# Index

Admiral of Holland—see
  Duivenvoorde, Jan van
Albrecht, Cardinal Archduke of
  Austria, 17, 22, 24, 85, 96
Algarve, 70, 99
Andalusia, 17, 54, 94, 96
Argosies, 70, 71
Armada of 1588, 9, 18, 21, 32,
  43, 50, 89, 96, 114, 117
Ashley, Antony, 11, 33, 44, 58,
  59, 87, 99, 111, 113

Barge, 54
Bark, 40, 42, 98, 99
Blount, Sir Christopher, 26, 35,
  64, 75, 80, 84, 86, 93, 100,
  119
Bodley, Sir Thomas, 101
Bouillon, Duke of, 23, 24, 25, 30

Cadiz, 52, 64, 68, 70;
  Counter-Armada at, 71–94;
  geography of, 58, 67, 75
Calais, citadel stormed, 22
Cape St. Vincent, 53, 56, 68,
  102, 112
Caravel, 65, 68, 70, 71, 92, 104
Carew, Sir George, 10, 11, 12,
  19, 26, 58, 59, 74, 89, 97, 118,
  119, 120, 121, 122, 170–173;
  Counter-Armada, 17–19, 21,
  29, 34, 37, 41, 44, 99–101,
  106, 109, 110, 113, 115; at
  Cadiz, 71–91; letters, 25, 30,
  44, 49, 59, 89, 115, 172;
  Journall, 124–158; wife, 13,
  91, 120, 122, 170, 172; family,
  11, 12, 19, 122
Carrack, 19, 103, 105
Cecil, Sir Robert, 10, 28, 109,
  119, 128; letters, 13, 25, 30,
  33, 38, 43, 44, 48, 49, 59, 89,
  114, 121
Cecil, William, Lord Burghley,
  10, 20, 22, 32, 43, 46, 97, 109,
  115
Christophero, Prince of Portugal,
  23, 40, 87, 100, 107
Clifford, Sir Conyers, 19, 23, 35,
  50, 80, 84, 93, 111
Council, Common , 19, 56;
  Privy, 10, 17, 22, 30, 34, 48,
  63, 89, 111, 114, 115;
  Selected, 10, 19, 52, 54, 56,
  58, 66, 68, 71, 76, 81, 85, 88,
  102, 103, 104, 109

Devereux, Robert, Earl of Essex,
  9, 57, 118, 119, 123;
  Counter-Armada, 10, 17, 20,
  21, 22, 25, 26, 29, 31, 32, 34,
  35, 40, 44, 46, 52, 53, 54, 55,
  58, 66, 68, 70, 99, 100, 102,
  103, 104, 105, 106, 108, 109,
  110, 111, 113, 118, 119, 123;
  at Cadiz, 71–93; letters, 26, 30,
  33, 48, 63, 108
Donne, John, 10, 20, 38, 55, 57,
  79, 87, 98

174

Doornik, Jan van, 21, 57, 65, 66;
Journal, 159–164
Dorrell, Marmaduke, 33, 44, 59,
65
Dover, 9, 17, 21, 23, 25–28, 38
Drake, Sir Francis, 18, 27, 30,
66–67, 98, 114
Dudley, Robert, Earl of
Leicester, 11, 18, 51, 60, 173
Dudley, Robert, 41, 51, 88
Duivenvoorde, Jan van, 9, 21,
42, 52, 56, 105, 113
Dutch officer accidentally killed,
102

Elizabeth I, Queen of England,
9, 11, 12, 15, 16, 22, 26, 30,
38, 43, 73, 171–173;
Counter-Armada, 17, 20, 27,
28, 32, 67, 89, 108, 109, 111,
114, 118, 119, 120, 121;
letters, 30, 31, 33, 47–48, 49,
63, 85, 105, 114, 116
Emanuel, Prince of Portugal, 23,
107

Faro, 99–102
Flyboat, 28, 39–42, 64, 65–66,
79, 95, 98, 99, 111, 115
Frigate, 78

Galleon, 9, 10, 42, 44, 65, 70,
71, 78–79, 118
Galley, 17, 22, 52, 56, 70, 71,
77, 78, 84, 85, 86, 92, 95, 97,
98, 99, 101
Garbrandtsz, John, 21, 42, 52,
56, 95
Gerrard, Sir Thomas, 35, 75, 80,
84, 93
Guezen (Sea-Beggars), 21

Hakluyt, 10
Hawkins, Sir John, 27, 30

Hawkins, Sir Richard, 27, 49
Henry IV, King of France, 22
Henry VIII, King of England,
11, 15, 18, 19, 87
Hilliard, Nicholas, 12, 171, 172
Howard, Charles, Lord of
Effingham, 9, 44, 106, 115,
118, 119; Counter-Armada, 10,
18, 20, 21, 22, 25, 27, 28, 30,
31, 32, 34, 38, 39, 44, 45, 46,
47, 52, 53, 54, 55, 56, 58, 67,
68, 70, 95, 98, 99, 100, 101,
102, 103, 104, 105, 110, 111;
at Cadiz, 71–93; letters, 11, 43,
93, 97, 108
Howard, Lord Thomas, 19, 25,
41, 43, 52, 65, 68, 70, 100,
106, 119, 121; at Cadiz, 75–88
Hoy, 26, 39, 40–42, 71, 99, 103
Hulk, 42

Knights of Cadiz, 87, 96

Leusen, Cornelius, 21, 42, 52, 56
Lord General—see Devereux,
Robert
Lords Generals—see Devereux,
Robert and Howard, Charles
Lord High Admiral—see
Howard, Charles
Lord Marshal—see Vere, Sir
Francis

Marbecke, Dr. Roger, 18, 47,
63, 90
Mascarenhas, Ferdinand Martins,
Bishop of Faro, 101
Master of Ordnance—see Carew,
Sir George
Measles, 99, 105
Medina Sidonia, Duke of, 84, 92,
93, 96, 97
Merkyrk, Baldwin, 34, 80, 92,
100, 101

Merrick, Gilly, 35, 88, 99, 111, 120, 123
Monson, William, 88, 107

Navigation, 45, 53, 56, 57, 58, 65, 72, 75, 107, 161

Perez, Antonio, 23, 24
Philip II, King of Spain, 16, 18, 22, 23, 24, 31, 38, 46, 48, 50, 52, 58, 73, 83, 84, 116
Pinnace, 42, 53, 71, 79, 80
Piracy, prizes, purchase, 20, 46, 47, 68, 70, 115
Plymouth, 9, 25, 26, 28, 29, 30, 35, 39, 48, 52, 54, 63, 65, 92, 99, 105, 106, 111, 113, 116
Puerto Real, 52, 68, 77, 78, 84, 95
Punishments, 29, 63, 74, 83, 102
Puntal, 77, 78, 80

Ragusan, 78, 95
Raleigh, Sir Walter, 10, 12, 18, 19, 25, 26, 29, 33, 38, 41, 43, 54, 58, 65, 105, 119, 172; at Cadiz, 71–89
Ransom, 83, 85, 86, 92, 101, 106
Rations, 36–37
Rear Admiral—see Raleigh, Sir Walter
Rear Admiral of Holland—see Leusen, Cornelius
Rota, 84, 92

Savage, Arthur, 34, 83, 105, 110

Secretary of the Council—see Ashley, Antony
Shakespeare, William, 13, 20, 45, 91, 120, 122
Ships, Lists of, English, 39–43, 166–169; Dutch, 42; Spanish, 78–79
Shooting, Art of, 60–63
Slingsby, William, 39, 51, 59
Smith, Captain, 35
Smith, Captain John, 32, 43, 73, 74, 75, 96
Spaniards in Cadiz, 78–82
Spoils, 46, 66, 90, 91, 101, 109–116, 161, 163
Sussex, Robert, Earl of, 35, 87, 93, 99

Vere, Sir Francis, 19, 23, 25, 26, 35, 40, 72, 77, 80, 89, 91, 93, 120
Vere, Horatio, 35, 86, 87, 92
Vice-Admiral—see Howard, Lord Thomas
Vice-Admiral of Holland—see Garbrandtsz, John
Victualler-General—see Dorrell, Marmaduke

Wagenaer, Lucas Jenszoon, 57
West, Thomas, 104
Weston, Richard, 66, 88
Wingfield, Sir John, 26, 35, 40, 77, 80, 82, 86, 92
Wingfield, Sir Richard, 26, 32, 35, 75, 92, 110